LEAVING

THE RAPTURE

BEHIND

LEAVING THE RAPTURE BEHIND

by Dr. Larry Pechawer

What the Bible *Really* Teaches
About the End Times

Leaving the Rapture Behind

published by MIREH Publishers

© 2003 by Larry Pechawer

International Standard Book Number: 0-9716369-1-0

Cover Design by Brian D. Rotert

MIREH Publishers
P. O. Box 1376
Joplin, MO 64802

www.leavingtherapturebehind.com

Table of Contents

Prologue:
Stranger Than Fiction

No one can question that the fictional *Left Behind* series has been wildly successful, not only in the Christian, but in the more general market. Sales for the end-times novels co-authored by Tim LaHaye and Jerry B. Jenkins now number in the tens of millions. Several full-length movies have been based on these as well, along with the usual spin-off marketing items. The tremendous impact of this current end-times emphasis upon our society cannot be questioned, either.

What *can* be questioned, however, is the claim of the authors that this fictional series is based upon the truths of what the Bible teaches about the end times. Many unwitting Christian readers know nothing else but the Rapture doctrine, or teachings concerning the fearful woes of the Great Tribulation to come after the Rapture. Their "blessed hope" is escaping earth before the evil "Antichrist" arrives on the scene. Fascinated by the imaginative unraveling of current events scenarios by the prophecy gurus, these believers have no clue as to how the Scriptures are actually being distorted by leading experts of this modern prophecy movement. These misrepresentations of what the Bible really says are done in order to make the Bible fit their questionable views on a host of subjects related to the return of our Lord. The "system," not the Scriptures, often takes precedence in the process of determining "what the Bible says" about the end times.

In a recent prophecy-oriented documentary of current events, *Are We Living in the End Times?*, Tim LaHaye wrote,

> That others before us were wrong about the nearness of the Lord's return should not deter us from searching the Scriptures, now

that some of the end-times prophecies are being unsealed. The ability to rightly evaluate the signs in our times is increasing almost daily, from Israel being reestablished as a nation, to the hatred of Israel by Russia and her Arab allies, to the emergence of China, and many other events– all part of the end-time prophetic tapestry. (p. xi)

Written prior to 9-11, these sentiments could use some updating. But that is the nature of the enterprise. Many of Hal Lindsey's earlier previous scenarios in his *The Late Great Planet Earth* later received extensive renovations by him in subsequent best-selling books.

One thing that you will notice immediately is that this present book is concerned about what the Bible says about these important end-times subjects, not what the Internet or newspapers say. This is a careful analysis of biblical teaching, not a current events primer. It intends to be informal, user-friendly and *absolutely relentless* in its exposure of the fallacies of the widely popular Rapture System. I believe that once the evidence from Scripture is carefully analyzed, the distinctive interpretive approach of Tim LaHaye, John MacArthur, Hal Lindsey and a host of other Christian authors will be found to be wanting, lacking solid credibility.

There are better answers to the questions raised concerning what the Scriptures teach than the ones we have been receiving from the huge array of end-times studies flooding the bookstores. You will find this work in your hands to be unlike anything else you have seen on the subject. It seeks to give solid answers to important questions. It strives to ask the right questions about many dubious practices in the current use of Scripture to support popular claims.

Too many studies on the end times that *claim* to be "Bible-based" actually only treat the text of Scripture in a superficial manner. Many authors love to pull verses out of context and plug them into the various sockets created by their particular system of interpretation. No group is more guilty of this than the many pop writers of the *pretribulational dispensational premillennial* persuasion. The *what?* you say? Some just call it dispensationalism, but there are important distinctions within that group that I will enumerate a bit later. In this book I'm just calling this whole approach the "Rapture System," so I don't have to keep writing you know what over and over again. I will also use the term "Rapturist" and "dispensationalist" interchangeably. The alleged Rapture of the church, separate from and prior to the Second Coming (or "Revelation") of Christ, is a key distinctive element of this interpretative system.

I will seek to avoid the tedious and often bewildering point- counter-point approach followed in many debate-structured works lately. Every effort has been made to represent the views of others fairly, without plodding to the point of distraction with endless documentation. This book is the beginning of a process, and more works are being planned in an effort to cover the wide range of critical topics that this whole last-things arena encompasses.

So why should we leave the Rapture behind? This book will attempt an informal but detailed explanation as to why the Rapture System should be rejected as an interpretative scheme. Along the way, lots of Scripture will be cited to allow readers to go at their own pace, some quickly getting the gist of the basic arguments, others slowly digging through the texts to try to build a bigger base of information to assess. Whatever your level of interest, whatever your level of commitment to a particular end-times perspective, I wish you well as you continue your journey in pursuit of knowing what the Bible really says about the end times. I believe that this book can be an important part of the evidence and information that you amass. The Lord's church is indeed living in important times with respect to the people God. But, then again, it always has.

1

AND THEN ALONG CAME EARL

I have vivid memories of my one summer factory job. Every college student should work in a factory at least one summer. Mine was especially memorable because of those hot, sultry afternoons in Maysville, Kentucky. Air conditioning? Not a chance. But that summer job was also memorable for another reason. I met a man who may have changed the direction of my life more than I have generally admitted to myself. His name was Earl.

A Different Classroom

Earl was one of the factory workers and a lay Baptist preacher. He was an older gentleman with an obvious love for God and His Word, and with a desire to serve Him. I've since forgotten Earl's last name, but his ideas about Bible prophecy are indelibly etched in my brain.

After a few days on the job, I learned of a Bible study during lunch in one of the storage rooms. The seating arrangement depended upon which part of the concrete floor suited your fancy. Earl usually led the discussion. I soon found out that my recent Bible college training put me at odds with many of the views bouncing around in that storage room. The bantering back and forth was generally good natured, but there came a point in time when, well let's just say things became counterproductive.

I had taken a class in Eschatology ("last things"), and I pretty much knew the basic millennial views. But I'd never encountered a real-live, flesh-and-blood, dyed-in-the-wool pretribulational dispensational premillennialist before. It was "prime time" and I was not quite so ready for it. With rapid succession, all the intricacies of the Rapture System began to unfold before me. It wouldn't take long on those occasions for me to start scratching my head, figuratively speaking. The Postponement of the Kingdom, the secret (yet noisy!) Rapture of the Church, the One Thousand Year Reign, the Great Tribulation—all bulwarks of dispensational theology. But also a part of the menu of things to swallow were the "second chance" for those who through unbelief missed Jesus the first time around (the "Rapture"), and the Gog and Magog revolt (Revelation 20:8) that really *isn't* the Gog and Magog invasion prophesied in Ezekiel 38-39. (It's a thousand years too late, according to the Rapture System. To be continued later....)

Digging In

What I came to realize was that I needed to know more of what "I believed" if I wanted to engage in meaningful dialogue with Earl and others like him. I had studied to the point where I was comfortable with what I myself believed, but it was now clear that I didn't have what it took to refute these dispensational teachings. Not that knowing more would necessarily have helped the situation, mind you. Once one's views on Bible prophecy are firmly entrenched, they tend to stay that way. The tinted glasses help filter out any rays of truth from outside sources.

Not always, though. Some of the champions of the amillennial position, for example, have been former Rapturists. Knowing pretribulational dispensational premillennialism inside-out *from the inside, then out* helped scholars like Philip Mauro (*The Hope of Israel, Seventy Weeks and the Great Tribulation*, etc.) and William E. Cox (*An Examination of Dispensationalism, Amillennialism Today, Biblical Studies in Final Things*) explain and refute effectively their former cherished beliefs.

It Just Can't Be!

Because of Earl, I studied matters I never would have otherwise. Two of his convictions about "rightly dividing the Word of Truth" stand out in my mind. I was shocked to find out that anyone could take the parallel accounts of Jesus' Olivet Discourse in Matthew 24, Mark 13 and Luke 21 and argue that, while Luke 21 was talking about the fall of Jerusalem in A.D. 70, Matthew 24 spoke about the so-called "Great Tribulation" after the "Rapture" of the church. It was inconceivable to me how Matthew 24 could be understood that way. After years of further reflection and study, it *still* is inconceivable.

First, from the standpoint of what Jesus actually said, it seems impossible to come up with a reasonable picture of how such a sermon could have unfolded. I cannot fathom how the same lengthy series of statements could have been spoken *twice*, once with reference to the first-century disciples (called "you") and the later with reference to the so-called "Tribulation Saints" (also called "you").

Second, one can only speculate why, upon the eve of His trial, crucifixion and resurrection experiences, Jesus would devote so much teaching to the plight of the "Tribulation saints" following the Rapture of the church. "And what do you mean by 'church,' anyway?" the twelve apostles might ask. If the dispensational treatment of the Olivet Discourse is correct, then Jesus didn't do His disciples any favors that particular day. What a confusing message. Instead, it is the Rapture System that is confusing on this point, as will be demonstrated later (see the chapters "Jesus and the End Times," I & II).

Another Doubtful Notion

Earl befuddled me with another interpretation of his that related to the "postponement theory." According to dispensationalism, Jesus came to establish the Kingdom, not the church. When that wicked generation rejected His message and claims, however, the Kingdom was allegedly postponed, and the church inserted temporarily in its place, a kind of "Plan B." After the supposed first-stage "Rapture" of the church, God will once again work with the Jewish nation to establish the Millennial Kingdom on earth, a kingdom that will be set up after the second stage "Revelation" of Christ, exactly seven years after the Rapture.

But exactly *when* was the kingdom "postponed"? Dispensational answers to that question are all over the map. Rapturists point to various junctures in Jesus' teaching ministry. Some of the parables are given as possible turning points. Jesus' condemnation of Jerusalem and its leaders in Matthew 23 is singled out by some interpreters. Others would mark out the crucifixion itself. Many would point to the Day of Pentecost on which the church was established (Acts 2).

Earl had a different solution, one that took me by total surprise. He pointed to the stoning of Stephen in Acts 7. It was at that point that the Sanhedrin, the official governing body of the Jewish nation, "officially" rejected the Gospel invitation and instead murdered its godly messenger. "Why was Jesus *standing* at the right hand of God, and not sitting?" Earl asked. I thought maybe it showed His interest in and concern for His faithful servant Stephen, who was about to become the first Christian martyr. Not so, I learned. Rather, Jesus was preparing to return to the earth in order to establish the Millennial Kingdom. Had the Sanhedrin accepted Stephen's invitation and embraced Jesus as their Messiah, Christ would have returned at that moment. They didn't, and instead stoned Stephen. Jesus sat down. The Kingdom was postponed.

Of course Earl's theory diminished the significance of Acts 2 beyond recognition. If the church wasn't established on the Day of Pentecost, what was? And how did the "whatever" founded then subsequently become the church for which Christ shed His blood? Lots of questions resulting from this dubious approach. No good answers.

Time To Move On

Those invigorating Bible studies at lunch took a turn for the worse, so it was decided that we study something that would not involve prophecy and the end times. So Genesis it would be. What a relief, I thought. My sense of repose lasted all of ten minutes, however. After all, the six days of creation each represent a thousand years, we were told, so after six thousand years the Millennium, the "seventh day," would arrive, and so on and so on. Reality now sunk in. There was no escape! I had to reassess the wisdom of my continued participation in the study. I chose to get off by myself at lunch and read my Bible, making the time more profitable for everyone concerned.

An important lesson I learned was that one's views on prophecy can be a big deal. They influence how Christians treat much of the Bible's teaching on a host of subjects, from Genesis One right on through. But as Francis Schaeffer has reminded us, the mark of the Christian is love, not a correct eschatological framework. Views on prophecy should not serve as a test of Christian fellowship, either.

However, issues involving the use of figurative language, the nature of the church, and the overall unity of the message of Scripture *are* extremely important. The "pro"-millennialists say that they're *all for* the Millennium, whatever it is! The "pan"-millennialists are convinced that it will all *pan out* in the end. Sorry, I don't have much use for either "view." I suspect that fuzzy thinking on the prophetic portions of the Bible may too often mean more of the same for the rest of God's Word.

Earl and I parted on good terms at the end of that summer. In fact I bought him a copy of *The Complete Works of Flavius Josephus* as a farewell gift. He'd been wanting to get one for some time. From Earl's side, I got a rejuvenated interest in theology, especially eschatology. My plans at that time were to enter graduate school as a Christian Ed major, but by the time school started it was Theology. A few months into the semester I realized that, as far as prophecy goes, Old Testament is "where it's at." And nearly thirty years later, it's where I'm still at.

My future studies involved matters more linguistic than theological. That was by design, since theology must come out of what the biblical text says. For me, the in-depth study of Hebrew, Aramaic and related languages seemed of paramount importance for achieving the best possible chance of correctly understanding and interpreting the Old Testament text. Too many of today's "prophecy experts" lack the ability to do serious biblical research. Some merely function as parrots of the teachings of others, who in turn have mimicked previous "authorities." It doesn't take long sorting through the piles and piles of recent end-times books to encounter the numbing redundancy many of those works contain.

I trust this book is different. I know it contains a few new, or nearly-new, wrinkles. I hope it helps rather than hinders the reader's understanding of what the Bible teaches about Christ's return and the end times. I am not writing for the scholarly audience, but I hope scholars may find some insights that prove useful. I have tried to make this book user-friendly so that as many Christians as possible may benefit from its contents.

The stimulation provided me by discussions with a factory worker/lay preacher named Earl was, in retrospect, a turning pint in my life. It is my prayer that the reading of this book may also be such a turning point for some of you. Whether you are locked into the Rapture System, looking for its holes, or just seeking answers, this book is dedicated to helping you better appreciate and understand the Bible's teaching for the Lord's church concerning the end times.

Postscript: The Scissors of the Lord

You are familiar with the phrase "Sword of the Lord" as a designation for the Scriptures. It is necessary now to introduce you to the "Scissors of the Lord"! Sounds contrived, perhaps, but actually these next several paragraphs are some of the most important in the entire book. Without them, you will be left with some puzzling questions and concerns.

Over and over in the following pages I point out the flaws and inconsistencies of the Rapture System (dispensationalism). The evidence, I believe, is compelling that dispensational teachers of biblical prophecy create a system that does not consistently represent the true meaning of the Bible as obtained by sound principles of interpretation. Words are taken out of context, entire passages are transported to times and settings not warranted by the obvious original setting. Fulfillments of prophecy described as such by *inspired* New Testament writers are often ignored, or minimized, because they are not literal enough to suit the system's standards. Therefore, a further, "double" fulfillment is sought for a yet future time, a fulfillment that will be in every way "literal."

Proof texts are pulled from the most unlikely spots and plugged into various theories or doctrines, and are presented as supporting evidence or proof for said doctrines. Throughout the book, I refer to this as the "cut-and-paste" method of biblical exegesis, hence the term Scissors of the Lord. This method is the dispensationalist's indispensable tool for "rightly dividing the Word of Truth."

But why do so many Bible students, teachers, and, yes, scholars feel that they need such a methodology for a tool? The answer is both simple and complicated. In a nutshell, practitioners wielding dispensational "scissors" are convinced that only an extremely literal approach to the interpretation of prophecy can save the church from drowning in subjectivism, antisupernaturalism, and unbelief. The rise of premillennial prophecy conferences in the late 1800's was in part a response to a growing liberalism and rise of unbelief in churches. Dispensational premillennialism was viewed as the only safe harbor from such inroads.

Even conservative scholars who employ non-dispensatioonal methodologies are viewed as suspect since they reject "the plain sense of Scripture" (as defined within dispensational guidelines). The amillennial view of prophecy, for example, is held by many conservative, Bible believing Christians. Yet it is soundly rejected because it recognizes the figurative nature of much of biblical prophecy (a significant portion of which is written, after all, in poetic style). According to the Rapture System, amillennialism was the step-child of early Roman Catholicism and was in part responsible for plunging the church into the Dark Ages. It is an unfair assessment, in my view, but that is how they choose to see it.

In short, the Scissors of the Lord are necessary to make the complex elements of a hyperliteral system fit together, context be hanged. And the system is necessary, because without it the church would eventually fall into the hopeless anarchy of subjective interpretation, and then damning unbelief. The key to understanding dispensational theology is to recognize it as representing a "fortress" mentality. Dispensational premillennialists see themselves as the guardians of faith and of a reliable Word from God. Just as the teachers of the Law of Jesus' day built a man-made "hedge" around the Law to protect it, modern dispensationalism employs the Scissors of the Lord to preserve a system of interpretation that seeks to protect the Bible as the literal Word of God. Any less "sure" method of reading Scripture may chip away at the authority of Scripture, so the dispensationalists feel.

As a result, an extensive, complex, "consistent" dispensational theology has developed. Its many fine points of clarification are tiresome to navigate through, since the system contains so many trouble spots inherent from the excessive literalism employed. And yet the proponents of the system agree to disagree at this level. It is the protective system itself that is non-negotiable. The Scissors of the Lord will always be necessary unless one can find his or her way out of the dispensational pre-millennial maze. That has proven possible for many, but it is not always an easy journey. Maybe this book can help.

2

THE MILLENNIAL MAZE

One of the real hindrances in coming to grips with prophetic issues is the oft-confronted "language barrier." Here we are referring to the formidable and frequently confusing terminology. Terms such as "Millennium," "Armageddon," "Great Tribulation," "Antichrist," "Rapture," and "First Resurrection" are but the tip of the iceberg. Probably the key challenge, however, is in understanding what the basic viewpoints indicate. What *is* an "amillenialist," anyway? How about a "pre-tribulational dispensational premillennialist?" Had enough? This chapter intends to be a (relatively) painless introduction to the basic millennial viewpoints.

The Language of Revelation 20

One's entire prophetic outlook is usually linked to his or her position concerning the "Millennium" in Revelation 20. This passage describes the "binding of Satan" and the reign of the departed saints with Christ. Satan's being bound and the saints' reigning with Christ are simultaneous events, each lasting a "thousand years" (Revelation 20:2-6). The word "Millennium" is actually the Latin word for "a thousand years," and is used by most Bible students to refer to this "thousand-year period" of binding and reigning.

An immediate observation to be made is that nowhere else in Scripture is such a thousand-year period described. The promises made in the Old Testament to Israel, for example, were always tied to the word "forever" (e.g., Isaiah 60:21–"they will possess the land forever"; Ezekiel 37:25–"David my servant shall be their prince forever"). It is true, of course, that the terms "forever" or "everlasting" in the Bible do not always convey the idea of eternity in the absolute sense. Often, "forever" must be interpreted within a given radius of time (just as we use "forever," "never," "always," etc. to describe aspects of our brief earthly life). In the Old Testament, slaves, if they so desired, could be attached to their Israelite masters "forever," i.e., as long as they lived. The Aaronic priesthood, the Sabbath, and circumcision are but several of the Old Testament institutions or practices that were to continue "forever," yet, according to the New Testament, have ended with Christ (Hebrews 7:11; Colossians 2:16, 17; Galatians 5:2-4). Usually context and further Scriptural revelation are the deciding factors for interpreting the term.

There is no hint in any Bible passage that Israel's "forever" promises will be fulfilled in a future one-thousand year period. A closer look at Revelation 20 further reveals that there is no mention of "Israel" in connection with the thousand-year reign of the saints. ("Those who had been beheaded because of their testimony for Jesus" are the ones reigning.) In light of what has been said, cautious reservation must accompany any attempt to link up the Old Testament "Golden Age" promises to Israel ("forever," not "millennial") with Revelation 20's millennial reign (involving martyrs for Christ, not "Israel").

Another important observation involving this passage is that the number "thousand" is often used in a non-literal sense elsewhere in Scripture. "Thousand" serves in Hebrew and Greek for the same effect that we achieve with "millions" and "billions" in modern speech. It can convey the idea of an indefinitely large number. Note the following: (1) "With the Lord a day is like a *thousand* years, and a *thousand* years are like a day" (2 Peter 3:8); (2) "For every animal of the forest is mine, and the cattle on a *thousand* hills" (Psalm 50:10); (3) "He is the faithful God, keeping his covenant of love to a *thousand* generations" (Deuteronomy 7:9). As a "complete" number, perhaps "thousand" serves more at times in the sense of a *qualitative,* rather than *quantitative* number. In light of the fact that Revelation is a book full of symbolic language, it would not be surprising to find the "thousand-year reign" of Christ representing an important (perhaps long) period of time without indicating an exact thousand-year period.

While interpretations vary regarding the actual duration of the "millennial" reign of Christ, further and more significant differences exist concerning when the "Millennium" occurs in relation to the Second

Coming of Christ. It is this relationship that is used to distinguish the various millennial views.

Note Well: It is a false conclusion to assume that the best eschatological viewpoint is the one that provides the most "natural" sense of Revelation 20. First, there is no basis for concluding that this is the most important text in all the Bible to consider. Who made it so? Why wouldn't the most natural interpretation of, say, Revelation 21-22 be just as important? Or of Matthew 24? Second, **the most "natural" interpretation of any text is suspect if it creates contradictions with the plain teaching of other texts!** A symbolic understanding of a particular word or verse may be necessary if it provides the best consistency in interpreting God's Word as a whole. What we do with Revelation 20 is, of course, important. But it is not the end-all and be-all of end-times study. And, for the record, *nobody* has a totally satisfactory treatment of this remarkable chapter.

Postmillennialism

Postmillennialists teach that the Second Coming will be postmillennial, that is, it will come *after* the "Millennium." Accordingly, they view the Millennium as occurring at the latter part of the church age. This Millennium, in their minds, will be a period of spiritual prosperity as the gospel of Christ is openly embraced by the majority of people in the world. Some postmillennialists would push the exactness of the "thousand-year" time frame, others would not. They would all agree, however, that this time period will be fulfilled by a triumphant church at a future time when "the earth shall be full of the knowledge of the Lord, as the waters cover the sea" (Isaiah 11:9).

When will this supposed glorious age begin? No one can say for sure. In fact, it may have already begun. Postmillennialists would draw the analogy of the change of seasons in the year or the transition, say, between the Middle Ages and the modern era. Only in retrospect can one say with confidence that a new day has dawned. Thus, as God's people look back, they will be able to pinpoint the time when the "Millennium" actually began. Universal peace and righteousness will characterize that glorious time.

The major problem with the postmillennial view is that there is little Scripture to support such a position. Although one must appreciate such an optimistic outlook (as one scholar said, "Don't you *wish* it were true?"), one finds no hard evidence for such a hopeful perspective. Frequently theology is fashioned according to social or cultural conditions. The postmillennial outlook was quite popular in the 1800's as that time period seemed to be pointing the way to great technological, medical, and educational advances. The potential of the new American frontier was fertile ground for the postmillennial perspective. Things *were* getting better, and the best seemed yet to come!

Few today, however, envision Christ's triumph over His enemies this side of the Second Coming. In light of two world wars, the Great Depression, the fearful nuclear age, ecological concerns, killer viruses, and now a day plagued by brutal dictatorships and fundamental Islamic terrorism, one can understand why such earlier optimism no longer captures man's imagination. Most feel divine intervention will be necessary. Postmillennialists have become a rare breed, although recent decades have witnessed some renewed interest in the approach. Neither the Bible nor current events seem to support this position.

Premillennialism

According to the premillennial view, the Second Coming will be "premillennial," meaning that it will come *before* the "Millennium." The church age will end with the Second Coming and a new age, the "Millennial Kingdom," will be ushered in. This will be a one-thousand-year earthly kingdom in which Christ reigns over His people. At the end of this period, Satan will be loosed for his "little season" and his armies, "Gog and Magog," will be destroyed by fire from heaven, while he himself is cast into the lake of fire (Revelation 20:7-10). At this point the "Great White Throne" judgment takes place (Revelation 20:11-15ff–an earlier "Sheep and Goats" judgment had supposedly earlier occurred at the Second Coming *before* the "Millennium"). Following this final judgment the Eternal State is ushered in.

It is crucial at this point to distinguish between the premillennialism described above from the view that most seem to hold to today. The view briefly described above is sometimes called the "historic" premillennial view, that brand of premillennialism which some Christians have adhered to throughout the centuries. Modern premillennialism, on the other hand, is characterized by several distinctive new features. This more recent viewpoint is also known as "dispensationalism." Although later chapters are devoted to the distinctive teachings of modern dispensationalism, a few remarks concerning this system need to be made at this juncture.

Dispensationalism (The Rapture System)

Dispensationalism teaches that God works with and tests man according to various divine "administrations." The popular *Scofield Reference Bible* distinguished between *seven* such "administrative periods" or "dispensations" (all Christians are "dispensational" to the extent that they at least recognize the distinction between the old and new covenants). According to dispensational premillennialism, the church age, God's current dispensation of grace, will be replaced in the future with the seventh and final dispensation, the Millennial Kingdom. Central in their thinking is the Jewish, nationalistic flavor of this kingdom. Christ came, according to them, to set up an earthly, Jewish kingdom (reminiscent of what those who rejected him were expecting!).

The Postponement Theory → the church is an afterthought?

When the Jews rejected their Messiah, so the view goes, the promised kingdom was "postponed" and in its place the church, a temporary stop-gap "parenthesis," was established. According to dispensational premillennialism, this promised kingdom will be established with a future Jewish generation (perhaps *already* living on earth) after God's dealings with the church are through. Accompanying this novel approach is the idea of a secret "Rapture" of the church prior to a Great Tribulation poured out against Israel. (This view seems to come from around 1830 in England and is generally credited to the Plymouth Brethren leader John Nelson Darby.) • This tribulation will be a prelude to Israel's salvation at the Second Coming. The Second Coming introduces the Millennial Kingdom in which the Jewish people, headquartered in Jerusalem, will be ruled by Jesus Christ as He sits on the "throne of David" in that city.

The Christians (both "raptured" and resurrected saints) technically *do not participate in the earthly Millennial Kingdom*. Their hope is different from Israel's. They perhaps view the millennial scene from their heavenly vantage point. God has two distinct peoples, dispensationalism stresses. Promises to Israel are *not* the same as promises to the church. At least that's what Rapturists teach.

Details of Debate

Earlier historic premillennialism always had those supporters who tended to emphasize Israel's role in the "Millennium." Excesses in this area eventually led to the birth of the dispensational approach described above. Actually, the earlier brand of premillennialism had its own problems and dispensationalism was an attempt to "smooth them out." The historic premillenial view had a problem with the "imminence" of Christ's return, since they saw so many "signs" that had to be fulfilled before the Second Coming. The dispensational "secret" Rapture solved that problem. All the signs were now placed between the Rapture and the later "Revelation" (or Second Coming). We will discuss those so-called "signs" a bit later.

The historic premillennial view has had a somewhat cloudy image of who would populate the millennial earth. It generally envisions a "mongrel" millennial society made up of those who enter the Millennium alive with their earthly bodies and those who come to life and enjoy their "resurrection" bodies at that time. Sounds like the "haves" and "have nots" to me.

Dispensationalism tidies things up a bit by shipping off most of the resurrected saints to heaven at the Rapture. Only the later "Tribulation saints," living or resurrected, will actually live upon the millennial earth. In making such distinctions, however, Rapturists seem to leave a worse mess of their own. Their distinction between a "Rapture" and the Second Coming (what they call the "Revelation"), separated by a supposed seven-year period, has given rise to a mind-boggling complex of last-days events, including a sequence of no less than *seven* distinct judgments. Their insistence upon an extremely literalistic manner of interpretation forces them to make unlikely distinctions. They distinguish between the future battles of "Armageddon" and "Gog and Magog" and then in turn conclude, due to "problems" with the timing created by their system, that the "Gog and Magog" battle of Revelation 20:7 must be a *different end-times battle* from the "Gog and Magog" battle of Ezekiel 38-39. You would think that one "Gog and Magog" would be enough!

A Flawed System

The dispensational brand of premillennialism has dangerous flaws in several regards. (1) Their hyperliteral interpretation leads to a bizarre, complex sequence of future events and ignores the way in which the New Testament interprets many of the Old Testament prophecies. (2) Their "postponement" theory teaches that Christ's church, rather than being central in God's plans, was merely an "afterthought" brought about by the Jewish rejection of the kingdom. (3) One might conclude that Christ, then, apparently *failed* in His mission when He came into the world, in that He came to establish the "Kingdom." (4) The separate "Rapture" of the church offers a *second chance* for those who are "left behind" then to accept Christ and enter the "Millennial Kingdom." *If, say, a hundred million or so Christians mysteriously vanished from the earth overnight* and you were "left behind," wouldn't *you* get right with God in a hurry?

Rapture Woe #1

The separate "Rapture" of the church offers a second chance for those who are "left behind" then to accept Christ and enter the "Millennial Kingdom."

A House Divided

The Major Division

At the most basic level, premillennialists are divided between historic and dipensational premillennialism. This division can be quite significant. A premillennnialist such as George E. Ladd (*Jesus and the Kingdom; The Blessed Hope*) can sound much more like an amillennialist than a dispensationalist. When the Rapturists' claim for "consistent" literalism in interpreting prophecy is scrutinized, the dispensational system quickly falls apart. Historic premillennialists make some of the best critics of the Rapture System.

It would be safe to assume that some 90% of modern "premillennialists" are dispensational in their perspective. This is true of Tim LaHaye,

Hal Lindsey, Grant Jeffrey and most other popular writers on the subject. They accept the notion of a separate Rapture of the church. While much more will be said later, enough has already been mentioned to indicate that there are serious implications from this system that must be carefully scrutinized. Unfortunately, the average "person in the pew" seems to be taken up (sorry) by this Rapture scenario. The system is promoted with the claim that it alone "takes God at His word." Makes sense to the unsuspecting.

While "historic" premillennialism, on the other hand, seems to contain fewer extremes, it also has its problems. It too must separate the Second Coming and the final judgment by a thousand-year period. It too suffers from a misunderstanding of how "Israel" relates to the church and how the word is used in the New Testament. It too depends upon a solitary, symbolic passage, Revelation 20, for developing a theological system centered upon a one-thousand-year earthly reign of Christ.

Major Dispensational Factions

Those who hold to the separate Rapture of the church form three camps within dispensationalism: the pre-tribulational dispensationalists, the mid-tribulational dispensationalists, and the post-tribulational dispensationalists. For a useful survey of the distinctive views involved, see *The Rapture: Pre-, Mid-, or Post-Tribulational?* (Archer, Feinberg, Moo, Reiter). The debate between these three positions quickly becomes tedious for the average reader. Unfortunately, all the debate is being carried out inside the dispensational "box." The issue relates to the timing of the Rapture in relation to the so-called Great Tribulation, and the basic dispensational assumptions about such concepts are shared by all involved. Many of the attacks leveled against the opponents are on target, but the solutions fall short of what is required for a valid alternative. By the time such a debate is digested, it becomes clear that what is being served is not all that satisfying. Both mid- and post-tribulationalists mount very good offenses against what I am terming in this work the Rapture System–pre-tribulational dispensational premillennialism.

Other Recent Rifts

It is ironic that at the very time more and more church-goers are jumping on to the traditional pre-trib Rapture bandwagon (led by La-

Haye, Lindsey, Walvoord, Ryrie, and others), many of the best and brightest within the dispensational fold are having second thoughts about some of the basic assumptions of that system. A new movement calling itself Progressive Dispensationalism is sending shockwaves throughout the Rapture System's realm. Scholars such as Craig Blaising, Darrel Bock, Robert Saucy and many others are muddying the waters that divide dispensational and non-dispensational viewpoints, much to the dismay of the classic dispensationalists. (Important works include Bock, *Progressive Dispensationalism*; Saucy, *The Case for Progressive Dispensationalism*; Herbert Bateman IV, ed., *Three Central Issues in Contemporary Dispensationalism*; and Blaising and Bock, eds., *Dispensationalism, Israel and the Church*.)

While maintaining Israel's special role in God's future plans, Progressive Dispensationalists by and large reject the sharp distinction between Israel and the church and the related Postponement Theory regarding the Kingdom. The church is today fulfilling Old Testament prophecies, according to them—a view to which Tim LaHaye and colleagues strenuously object. Progressive Dispensationalism is truly a "work in progress." Just where these scholars will eventually land remains uncertain. They have rejected some of the key foundations for the Rapture theory. By doing so, these scholars would seem to be in a temporary no-man's land. At present they are being severely criticized by many traditional pre-trib Rapturists.

For some time now, the current leadership at Dallas Theological Seminary, including President Charles Swindoll, has been trying to tone down some of the old-time dispensational rhetoric there and soften the pre-trib emphasis. And now a number of Dallas faculty have joined the Progressives. Criticisms from classic dispensationalists have been pointed. "Dallas ... we have a problem!"

Other variations have emerged, a testimony to the fact that even more feel that the Rapture System is "broken" and needs fixing. Marvin Rosenthal, for many years the director of The Friends of Israel Gospel Ministry, broke ranks with the pre-trib convictions of his overseers and supporters to promote a new wrinkle of the mid-tribulational view he outlined in his 1990 book, *The Pre-Wrath Rapture of the Church*. His agonizing decision to do so eventually cost him his job, and, to date, his new views have not generated the response he had hoped for. But they add to the overall picture of dispensationalism as truly a "house divided."

Amillennialism

Last, but (in our view) not least, is the amillennial view. The prefix *a-* indicates negation, therefore the term "non-millennial" could properly be used. It is not that amillennialists do not believe that such a period described as the "thousand-year reign" exists. Rather, they just do not view it as a literal thousand-year period.

The Thousand Years, not Literal but Now

Remember our earlier listing of several references where "thousand" served as a symbolic number: "With the Lord a day is like a *thousand* years, and a *thousand* years are like a day" (2 Peter 3:8); "For every animal of the forest is mine, and the cattle on a *thousand* hills" (Psalm 50:10); "He is the faithful God, keeping his covenant of love to a *thousand* generations" (Deuteronomy 7:9). Some have preferred the term "historical millennial," but that is a bit unwieldy, so the normal term will be retained here.

Amillennialists do not believe that other Scriptures support the (premillennial) contention that an earthly "Millennium" will follow the Second Coming. Nor do they feel, however, that such a period fits well at the end of the church age as the postmillennialists teach. They maintain that the "thousand years" symbolism of Revelation 20 logically fits into *a period of time already known from Scripture*. They equate the "thousand years" with the entire church age. Is this view, the reign of Christ with His saints is a *present* reality.

Satan Now "Bound" in a Real Sense

The "binding of Satan," according to this approach, is also a present reality. Through Christ's victorious resurrection over death, and through the subsequent preaching of the gospel, Satan in a real sense is "bound." This "binding" need not be absolute, but could convey the notion of limitation. Reference to several of the following Scriptures will show the idea that Christ's victory over Satan has already taken place: Genesis 3:15; Hebrews 2:14-15; I John 3:8; Matthew 12:29 (note the same word "bind");

Luke 10:17-18; John 12:31-32. For example, Hebrews 2:14-15, in speaking of Christ's first coming, says,

> Since the children have flesh and blood, he too shared in their humanity so that by his death he might destroy him who holds the power of death–that is, the devil–and free those who all their lives were held in slavery by their fear of death.

Or take 1 John 3:8.

> He who does what is sinful is of the devil, because the devil has been sinning from the beginning. The reason the Son of God appeared was to destroy the devil's work.

In a very real sense, then, Satan is now "destroyed"; his *work* is now "destroyed" (or "rendered powerless"). In a very real sense, he is now "bound." Clearly, limitation, not absolute powerlessness, is what is involved here. I know that this doesn't jive with Hal Lindsey's *Satan is Alive and Well on Planet Earth*, but I believe that it is what the Bible teaches.

Note Well: Rapturists also have a problem with the binding of Satan. According to their understanding of the events during the Millennium, many millions (those allegedly born during the Millennium) will reject Christ's reign, even though His visible presence will result in unimaginable blessings for all. Millions of "closet rebels" will be chafing at the bit, and Satan's release will be a welcome development in their desire to throw off Christ's shackles. According to Revelation 20, Satan's binding was so that he might not "deceive the nations." Apparently, however, Satan's being "bound" doesn't stop millions all over the world from rejecting Christ's millennial reign, does it? In what sense, by literal dispensational standards, would the nations then not be deceived?

Further Matters

Amillennialists do not all agree on whether Satan's "little season" chronologically terminates the "Millennium," or whether it refers to the nature of Satan's limited, temporary influence over individual Christians during that time (in contrast with the glorious "thousand-year reign"). All are in agreement, however, that the Second Coming *follows* the "Millennium" and that the "thousand years" are symbolic of the present church age. Most who hold this view would link the glorious "Golden Age" prophesied in the Old Testament *not* with the "Millennium," but with the Eternal State–"the New Heaven and New Earth" (Revelation 21:1).

Amillennialists claim that their view best allows the New Testament teachings to be the guiding factor. Dispensationalists, on the other hand, tend to use highly subjective interpretations of Old Testament prophetic texts to serve as their basis for interpreting the New Testament. I am convinced that the amillennial method of interpretation offers the best chance for a reasonable, consistent understanding of the entire revelation of God. The picture in the Gospels and epistles is that of a single, climactic, final return of our Lord. As well, amillennialists rightly point out *the conspicuous absence of any promise of a future earthly Jewish kingdom anywhere in the New Testament.*

A Disputed Subject

Clearly there is a disagreement between groups of believers on the "millennial" issue. Sometimes the debate can become rather heated. Should such be the case? Should the issue be a source of division for Christians? Can this be avoided?

Some, frankly, would refuse to wear any of the above labels. At least one scholar has called himself a "pro-millennialist." He was not sure what the proper understanding of the Millennium should be, but whatever it is, he was all for it! Another preferred the term "pan-millennialism." He was confident that it would all "pan out" in the end!

We are partly sympathetic with the above sentiments and do not feel that such issues should be tests of fellowship or sources of division. However, neither do we feel that one can avoid taking and maintaining a basic viewpoint. The options are clearly limited; the ramifications of the choices can be rather significant. John F. Walvoord, in his *The Return of the Lord* (p. 46), states, "The dispensational premillennial return of Christ is *not an insignificant matter,* but is a very important doctrine. It is the *key that unlocks* the great treasures of the prophetic word; it *sets everything in its right perspective* ..." (*italics* mine). Unfortunately, in our opinion, some use their millennial views as their theological starting point. A perspective so derived can become hopelessly imbalanced.

The following chapters are an attempt to allow the Scriptures to speak for themselves on this timely topic. Are the Lindseys, Walvoords and LaHayes of our day correct in their assessment that the Postponement Theory, Rapture, and earthly Millennium are the keys that unlocks God's word? Or does the answer lie elsewhere? Could, in fact, the vast majority of writers and speakers in this area today be fundamentally wrong on key issues? The intention of this book is to demonstrate just that. It's time for the church to leave the Rapture doctrine behind and move on.

Postscript: Beware the Preterists

In part because of the excesses of many popular futuristic schemes, including the Rapture System, another approach has raised its ugly head. The term "preterist" simply refers to the "past" or "historical," and as such can serve as a useful term at times. However, the prophetic system known as full "Preterism" is an unwelcome addition to the controversy, in my view. Several books are now available featuring debates between preterists and dispensationalists. Once such book is *The Great Tribulation: Past or Future?* (1999), by Thomas Ice (dispensational) and Kenneth L. Gentry Jr. (preterist). I cannot recommend such books except to serious students of the field. The approaches presented are from opposite extremes, with the middle ground being altogether ignored. It is like an ancient mariner in Greek mythology having to choose between the monsters Scylla and Charybdis, rather than being able to navigate a safe course well between them.

Unlike the futuristic excesses of the Rapture System, preterism teaches that Second Coming prophecies have all *already been fulfilled* in connection with the A.D. 70 destruction of Jerusalem. That is when the Son of Man came in "great power and great glory with his holy angels." No kidding! Preterists emphasize the "now," "near," and "at hand" language in various promises of Jesus' return and claim that the only way to keep our Lord and His apostles from being discredited is to conclude that Jesus did come "soon"–in A.D. 70.

I have taught Old Testament in Bible college for over two decades now, so I understand their arguments about apocalyptic language–"stars falling," "moon turning to blood," etc.–being used at times for temporal events (e.g., the fall of Babylon, Assyria, or some other empire). But this system takes the concept beyond the limits of good sense. It is difficult to see how the Great White Throne judgement, or the Sheep and Goats judgement, or the creation of the New Heaven and New Earth, or the meeting Him in the clouds could have transpired in A.D. 70. Those speculations takes more "faith" than I'm willing to invest in an interpretive scheme. Like many packages offered out there, this system can sound good on the surface. There are just too many holes to patch up. I intend to analyze the preterist view in greater depth in an upcoming book, *The Man of Lawlessness and the Time of the End*. For now, let me speak plainly: *Beware the preterists.*

Rapture Woe #2

The "postponement" theory teaches that Christ's church, rather than being central in God's plans, was merely an "afterthought" brought about by the Jewish rejection of the kingdom. One might conclude that Christ, then, apparently failed in His mission when He came into the world, in that He came to establish the "**Kingdom.**"

Rapture Woe #3

Rapturists' hyperliteral interpretation leads to a bizarre, complex sequence of future events and ignores the way in which the New Testament interprets many of the Old Testament prophecies.

Rapture Woe #4

At the very time more and more church-goers are jumping on to the traditional pre-trib Rapture bandwagon, many of the best and brightest within the dispensational fold are having second thoughts about some of the basic assumptions of that system. A new movement calling itself Progressive Dispensationalism is sending shockwaves throughout the Rapture System's realm.

3

ISRAEL AND THE CHURCH

In light of the previous remarks regarding the Rapture System, the question of the relationship between Israel and the church must be addressed. Many who view a future restoration of national Israel to Palestine see the church as an interruption, rather than the fulfillment of God's plans for Israel. George E. Ladd defines this Israel-church distinction as the "heart" of the dispensational system. In dispensationalism, the church is viewed as a mere "parenthesis" in God's true plan for Israel, a "mystery" about which the Old Testament was absolutely silent. The following study will refute this artificial distinction, however, as it portrays the proper relationship the church enjoys with Israel and with Old Testament prophecy.

The Church in Relation to Israel

In light of dispensational attempts to contrast Israel and the church, it is necessary to emphasize briefly the Jewish nature of the church. At its inception, the church made up of believers in Christ was a Jewish institution. Gentiles were later incorporated into it on an equal basis. While dispensationalists push the concept of a "Gentile church," Jesus actually manifested a Jewish-Gentile church. The apostles were Jews, the New Testament writers were Jews (with the possible exception of Luke), the three thousand converted at Pentecost were all Jews. The early chapters of Acts describe a Jewish church. Several years later it is reported that many myriads ("ten thousands") of the Jews had believed (Acts 21: 20). Some today estimate that during the first century A.D. there were over one million Jewish converts to Christianity, with the number going as high as two million. In any case, many thousands of Jews embraced

Jesus–Yeshua–as their Messiah. This being the case, it would be perfectly natural to view the church as the fulfillment of promises given to Israel.

Robbing Israel?

The accusation is frequently made that amillennialists and other non-dispensationalists are "robbing" Israel of its promises by applying them to the church. In light of the apparent confusion among certain groups concerning the proper relationship between Israel and the church, the present remarks will attempt to clarify the issue.

First of all, it is somewhat misleading to state as does Bernard Ramm, "The amillenarians believe that the prophecies made to Israel are fulfilled in the church" (*Protestant Biblical Interpretation*, p. 257). Here one must distinguish between God's unfolding plan of redemption in history and the final eternal (or "eschatological") consummation. The church age is a glorious phase in God's program in history that is often predicted by the prophets. The ultimate hope of Israel, as well of all nations, however, is the final consummation. The church age and the Eternal State are often blended together in prophecy because of the special prophetic perspective that united the first and second comings of Christ. The hope of Old Testament saints is *shared* by the New Testament church, not fulfilled in it. Regarding Jews after the cross, however, the Scriptures clearly teach that it is only through the church of the risen Lord that Israel according to the flesh can receive salvation and the promise of eternal life. Summing up, the church is a more glorious phase of Israel's redemption, and the prophecies that point ahead to Christ's first coming and the establishing of the church also preview the ultimate result of that first coming–His Second Coming to usher in the glorious Eternal State.

Remnant Israel

Another necessary point to make is that Israel and the church should not be considered as exact counterparts. It is not an "either-or" proposition. "Israel" as used in Scripture can denote not only the physical nation itself, but also the spiritual remnant *within* that nation. Paul said, "It is not as though God's word had failed. For not all who are descended from Israel are Israel" (Romans 9:6). Not all Jews, according to Paul, were "true Jews."

> A man is not a Jew if he is only one outwardly, nor is circumci-
> sion merely outward and physical. No, a man is a Jew if he is one
> inwardly; and circumcision is circumcision of the heart, by the Spirit,
> not by the written code. Such a man's praise is not from men, but
> from God. (Romans 2:28-29)

The church, on the other hand, is by definition composed only of the
spiritual remnant who accept Christ as their Savior. Paul quotes from
Isaiah,

> Isaiah cries out concerning Israel: "Though the number of the
> Israelites be like the sand by the sea, only the remnant will be saved."
> (Romans 9:27, from Isaiah 10:22)

This spiritual remnant is composed of "remnant Israel" existing after
the cross, along with the elect remnant of *Gentiles* who embrace Israel's
Messiah. While God's promises of blessing in the Old Testament for physical Israel are valid only for the obedient, the remnant, the promises to the
church are, by definition, addressed only to the remnant–those who have
entered into a New Covenant relationship with God in Christ. Regarding
physical Israel after the cross, its salvation hinges upon its relationship to

Rapture Woe #5

**Paul taught that a "remnant" from Israel–the
elect throughout the ages–would be saved,
not some future generation after the Rapture
of the church.**

its Messiah. The distinction then is not between Israel and the church,
but rather between Old Testament remnant Israel and New Testament
remnant Israel. Just as the Old Testament remnant contained not only
physical Jews but also some proselytes ("spiritual Jews," or foreigners who
embraced the God of Israel; see Isaiah 56:6; note also Rahab, Ruth), so
too the New Testament remnant contains not only Israel according to
the flesh, but also Gentiles who together accept Israel's Messiah. The
conditions of the old covenant have been replaced by those of the new,
never to return–not after an alleged Rapture; not during an alleged Jewish
kingdom on earth.

Summing up, the prophetic future of Israel in history is, to an extent, fulfilled in the church, the New Testament "Israel of God" (Galatians 6: 16). This embraces much of Messianic prophecy that points to the establishment of a New Covenant Israel. Those prophecies, however, that view the ultimate, eternal restoration of Israel are not *fulfilled* in the church age, but are properly *applied* to the church–God's present faithful remnant–who will share in them with the remnant of Old Testament saints. The New Heavens and New Earth and the New Jerusalem (Revelation 21-22) represent (old covenant and new)"Israel's" eternal reward.

The Church As the Fulfillment of Old Testament Prophecy

The dispensational approach to the New Testament betrays the real weaknesses of the entire Rapture System. The claim is made, one that can only be sustained by perverting the clear meaning of many passages, that the New Testament does not support the amillennial position that the church is the fulfillment of Old Testament prophecy. John F. Walvoord boldly asserts:

> The general context of the New Testament is entirely in favor of the premillennial viewpoint. The amillennial interpretation has not one verse of positive testimony in the New Testament and can be sustained only be spiritualizing the prophecies of the Old Testament as well as the teaching of the New.[1]

The Hope of Israel

Upon examining the New Testament itself, however, it becomes evident that the inspired apostles themselves "spiritualized" many Old Testament prophecies.

Amillennialist Philip Mauro cites Acts 26:6-7 to show the vital connection between the church and Israel's prophetic hope. Paul before Agrippa said:

> And now it is because of my hope in what God has promised our fathers that I am on trial today.This is the promise our twelve tribes

---

[1] John F. Walvoord, "The Historical Context of Premillennialism," *Bibliotheca Sacra* 108 (April, 1951), 158-59.

are hoping to see fulfilled as they earnestly serve God day and night. O king, it is because of this hope that the Jews are accusing me.

Mauro concludes:

> This is very definite. It proves that Paul, in preaching the gospel of Christ crucified and risen from the dead, was proclaiming to the people of Israel the fulfillment of God's promise to that people .... (*The Hope of Israel*, p. 26)

Paul further maintained in the presence of Agrippa that his message of Christ's crucifixion, resurrection, and offer of salvation to the Gentiles proclaimed exactly "what the Prophets and Moses said was going to take place" (Acts 26:22-23). In urging Agrippa to accept Christ as his Lord and Savior, Paul appealed to the direct testimony of the prophets: "King Agrippa, do you believe the Prophets?" (Acts 26:27). Certainly Paul did not believe that the Old Testament was silent about the present reign of Christ in the church age! Rather, he viewed this subject as its *central theme*.

In his letter to the Romans, Paul again declared that the gospel of Christ's birth from the seed of David and resurrection as the Son of God was "promised beforehand through His prophets in the holy Scriptures" (Romans 1:1-4). His message of proclamation was in fact "the good news of the promise made to the fathers" (Acts 13:32).

The Witness of the Prophets

Jesus Himself evidently saw His crucifixion, resurrection, and ascension as matters of prophetic fulfillment. Accordingly he maintained that if the two on the road to Emmaus had believed "all that the prophets had spoken," they would have realized that it was necessary "for Christ to suffer these things and to enter into His glory" (Luke 24:25-26).

Dispensationalists maintain with great difficulty the premise that the conversion of the Gentiles in the New Testament is *not* the fulfillment of the conversion promised in the Old Testament. *Rather, they claim, the Old Testament was totally silent about the church age and spoke of a Gentile conversion in connection with the so-called Millenium.* The conversions recorded in the New Testament were only "in harmony" with God's later promised plans. If such a position were true, it would be hard to escape the conclusion that Paul himself was totally confused.

Rather, Paul saw his mission to the Gentiles as the fulfillment of Old Testament prophecy. In fact, his turning to the Gentiles was God's "command": "For thus the Lord has commanded us, 'I have placed you as a light for the Gentiles, that You should bring salvation to the end of the earth'" (Acts 13:47, citing Isaiah 49:6). His ministry was in direct obedience to the heavenly vision he had received (Acts 26:19-20), and was in direct fulfillment of Old Testament prophecy:

> But I have had God's help to this very day, and so I stand here and testify to small and great alike. I am saying nothing beyond what the prophets and Moses said would happen–that the Christ would suffer and, as the first to rise from the dead, would proclaim light to his own people and to the Gentiles. (Acts 26:22-23)

Paul viewed the conversion of the Gentiles as Christ's confirmation of "the promises given to the fathers" (Romans 15:8-12). Cited are such "Gentile" passages as Psalm 18:49; Deuteronomy 32:43; Psalm 117:1; and Isaiah 11:10. In discussing the stumbling of Israel and the blessings upon the Gentiles resulting from the cross, Paul cites the prediction of Moses: "I will make you jealous by that which is not a nation, by a nation without understanding will I anger you" (Romans 10:19, citing Deuteronomy 32:21). Similarly he refers to Isaiah: "I was found by those who sought me not, I became manifest to those who did not ask for me" (Romans 10:20, citing Isaiah 65:1). For a man who viewed the Old Testament as being "absolutely silent" about the church age, Paul certainly had a strange way of quoting Old Testament prophecies!

One Nation Under God

~ The account found in Acts 10 concerning the household of Cornelius is also conclusive in this regard. Peter, sent there to preach by divine command, spoke what were to be the concluding remarks of his message: "Of Him *all the prophets bear witness* that through His name every one who believes in Him has received forgiveness of sins" (Acts 10:43). While he spoke the very words, the Holy Spirit fell upon that Gentile audience, dramatically signaling the beginning of the inclusion of Gentiles into the church. It is clear then that the prophets "bore witness of" the church itself. The same Holy Spirit who gave the prophetic utterance dramatically confirmed it.

It is apparent that Paul believed that the Old Testament rite of circumcision has been replaced by "the circumcision of Christ" (Colossians 2:11-13; also Galatians 5:6; 6:12-15; Ephesians 2:11; Philippians 3:2-3, etc.). Moreover, nowhere in the New Testament does it even suggest that circumcision will ever be re-instated in God's economy. The obvious conclusion is that "Israel according to the flesh" has been replaced from the covenant relationship by spiritual Israel, the church of Jesus Christ. When Paul addresses the church as "the Israel of God" (Galatians 6:16), he supports such a position.

(It is a matter of debate and no little consternation among dispensationalists as to which *old covenant practices* will be re-instituted by the saints during the alleged Millennial Kingdom. Because of their commitment to extreme literalism, many dispensationalists conclude that animal blood sacrifices will once again be offered in the Millennium. This remarkable view is based on the temple vision in Ezekiel 40-48. These animal offerings will be "memorials" of Jesus' death, not anticipatory, as were those in the Old Testament. And yet Ezekiel describes them as "atoning" sacrifices [e.g., Ezekiel 45:22]. So much for literalism there! Rapturists claim that their views are based on a *consistent literal interpretation*. Many examples in this present book will show that they are *not*.)

In Ephesians 2, Paul's argument is conclusive for the view that the church now shares in the prophetic promises for Israel. Those prophecy "experts" who would arbitrarily distinguish between Israel's "national" and "individual" promises certainly must find grave difficulties with this passage. The Old Testament saints who were saved (recipients of "individual promises") share in the same hope that New Testament saints share, while a single future generation of Jews will share in the "national" promises, allegedly. Paul, however, sounds very "nationalistic" when he offers Gentiles in the church full "citizenship" in Israel. His argument contains useful parallels of thought. Those who were formerly unsaved Gentiles were: (1) "separate from Christ"; (2) "excluded from the commonwealth of Israel"; (3) "strangers to the covenants of promise"; (4) with "no hope and without God in the world" (Ephesians 2:12). Now, however, in Christ Jesus they have seen "brought near by the blood of Christ" (Ephesians 2:13). Paul explains,

> For he himself is our peace, who has made the two one and
> has destroyed the barrier, the dividing wall of hostility by abolishing

> in his flesh the law with its commandments and regulations. His purpose was to create in himself one new man out of the two, thus making peace, and in this one body to reconcile both of them to God through the cross, by which he put to death their hostility.
>
> (Ephesians 2:14-16)

Therefore, to the Gentiles Paul promises, "So then you are no longer strangers and aliens, but you are fellow-citizens with the saints, and are of God's household" (Ephesians 2:19). The necessary conclusion from Paul's argument in Ephesians 2 is that, through Christ, Gentiles are now part of "the commonwealth of Israel" and sharers in "the covenants of promise," for they are now "fellow-citizens" of God's household. The church shares in the prophetic hope of what was formerly national Israel.

We have a choice to make here. We can base our understanding of the relationship between Israel and the church on the teachings of Scripture, or we can base it on the ever-fluid landscape of current events. Recent history shows that the political scenarios and date-settings of dispensational gurus have been wrong time and time again. Apologies for misleading the Christian community are conspicuously absent. Instead, we are urged to get the updated forecast, and an unwitting church keeps tuning in.

Israel and the Land of Promise

The dimensions of the promised land are first recorded in Genesis 15:18 as being "from the river of Egypt as far as the great river, the river Euphrates." The boundaries are further marked out in Exodus 23:31; Number 34:1-12; Deuteronomy 11:24; and Joshua 1:4. H. A. Ironside comments regarding these boundaries:

> Israel never possessed that much of the land. Even in the day of King Solomon, the land Israel possessed was not so great as that here promised to Abraham. So I take it that in the coming day, God will confirm this promise. (*The Lamp of Prophecy*, p. 73)

A Past Possession

Dispensationalism teaches that the land promised to Israel has not yet been entirely possessed. It can be easily shown, however, that in fact Israel *did actually possess* the land promised, so that, as Philip Mauro states, "nothing remains, of the promise we are considering, for fulfillment to a reconstituted Jewish nation" (*The Hope of Israel*, p. 70). The land Joshua was commanded to possess was the entire promised land (Joshua 1:3, 4). It is true that they did not immediately conquer the entire land. Mauro states that they were "constructively in possession of the whole land of promise" as they crossed the Jordan. God told them He would drive out their enemies "little by little" so that they could properly control the land (Exodus 23:23, 30). Some groups, of course, were not driven out because of the lack of faith on Israel's part (Joshua 15:63; 16:10; 17:12). Jerusalem was not captured until the time of David. For all intents and purposes, however, the possession of the land was accomplished in Joshua's day; and certainly there is no looking ahead in the Bible to a modern-day fulfillment. As Joshua 21:43-45 says,

> So the LORD gave Israel all the land he had sworn to give their forefathers, and they took possession of it and settled there. The LORD gave them rest on every side, just as he had sworn to their forefathers. Not one of their enemies withstood them; the LORD handed all their enemies over to them. Not one of all the LORD's good promises to the house of Israel failed; every one was fulfilled.

It is also clear in Scripture that Israel actually did possess *literally* all of the land promised, even to the Euphrates River. David is described as having restored his rule at the River, i.e., the Euphrates (2 Samuel 8:3; 1 Chronicles 18:3). Also, "Solomon ruled over all the kingdoms from the River to the land of the Philistines and to the border of Egypt ..." (I Kings 4:21). In fact, he had dominion over "everything west of the River" (I Kings 4:24). Clearly, then, there is no need for a further fulfillment of the promise to Abraham with regard to possession of territory. The promise has been completely fulfilled. (One hint: When looking at a map, think of the Euphrates as more of a *northern* boundary, since the vast Arabian desert served to mark off the eastern limits. This desert was *not* part of what Abraham was promised.)

A Conditional Possession ～

Speaking to Abraham of "all the land which you see," God promised, "I will give it to you and to your seed forever" (Genesis 13:15). The question must be asked, "How long is *forever?*" Ironside states simply, "The term 'forever' means *forever*, as long as the world stands." This, however, is a shallow conclusion for such a rich concept. The fulfillment of this promise can be approached in at least three ways. (1) Being a conditional promise, in light of passages such as Deuteronomy 7:9-10, it was *not* fulfilled, on account of disobedience, in which case the meaning of 'OLAM, "forever," is not crucial in regard to the physical inhabitance of Palestine. (2) In the absolute sense of "eternal," 'OLAM could refer to the eternal blessings of the faithful "seed," both Jew and Gentile, thus being an expression for heaven. (3) The use of "forever" may be limited by a recognized parameter. In his book, *Biblical Studies in Final Things*, William Cox devotes a chapter to the meaning of "everlasting." He states,

> "Everlasting" or "eternal" as used in the Scriptures must be interpreted according to the radius of time included in a particular promise. In other words, like all other scriptures, these words must be interpreted according to their context. A promise was "eternal" or "everlasting" for the duration of time God decreed to use a given method of dealing with his people. (*Biblical Studies in Final Things*, p. 96)

In 2 Chronicles 7:16 God promised to live in Solomon's house "forever," i.e., "as long as the house stood." In many passages (e.g., Exodus 40:15, Numbers 25:13) we are told that the house of Aaron was to be an "everlasting" priesthood. Hebrews makes it clear that the Aaronic priesthood ended with Jesus Christ, our High Priest. Therefore "the priesthood of law was everlasting only as long as the law was in effect." In discussing the phrase "and unto thy seed forever" (Genesis 13:15) Adam Clarke says that

> ... this was always the design of God, not that Abram himself should possess it, but that his posterity would, till the manifestation of Christ in the flesh. And this is chiefly what is to be understood by the words forever, *ad 'olam*, to the end of the present dispensation, and the commencement of the new. (*Commentary and Critical Notes*, I, p. 95)

Regarding the expression "everlasting possession" (Genesis 17:8), Clarke writes:

> Here 'OLAM appears to be used in its accommodated meaning, and signifies the completion of the Divine counsel in reference to a particular period or dispensation. And it is literally true that the Israelites possessed the land of Canaan till the Mosaic dispensation was terminated in the complete introduction of that gospel .... (p. 110)

In the same way, circumcision as an "everlasting" covenant was made void at the birth of the church. Paul stated that "if you receive circumcision, Christ will be of no benefit to you" (Galatians 5:2). If one looks at the terminology of the land promises in this light, one can say that the promise indeed has been literally fulfilled.

A Forever Possession

One final point should be made concerning those who feel a literal thousand-year reign of Christ on earth is necessary that "forever" might literally be fulfilled, i.e., "as long as the earth exists." Most who see the modern nation of Israel as a part of the fulfillment of prophecy also feel that the Millennium is very near. What is curious in this scheme of things is that, in their effort to get another thousand years to help fulfill their concept of "forever," these scholars conveniently forget the 1900 years when the Jews were scattered (and incidently, *most still are*). So this view postulates approximately 1500 years of possession, 1900 years scattered, and 1000 years again of possession. In what way will an earthly millennium solve the problem of "forever"?

It is claimed that the millennial earth will not be radically altered, but will rather effortlessly merge into the eternal New Earth. Therefore the land promise is "forever." Yet Peter wrote, "But the day of the Lord will come like a thief. The heavens will disappear with a roar; the elements will be destroyed by fire, and the earth and everything in it will be laid bare" (2 Peter 3:10). Sounds like a pretty radical change to me. When "possessing the land forever" is given as part of Israel's messianic hope in Scripture, it would seem best to link that with the scene in Revelation 21-22 and understand it as fulfilled in the eternal New Creation that God has promised His people—the New Jerusalem resting on the New Earth.

The Seed of Abraham

The patriarchal land promises have both a physical and spiritual aspect. The physical aspect pertains to Abraham's earthly seed, his physical descendants. With regard to Ishmael, Abraham would be the father of many nations. With regard to Isaac, he would be the father of a great nation with descendants as numerous as the dust of the earth (fulfilled, as seen in 1 Kings 4:20: "sand of the seashore"), and as the stars in the heavens (fulfilled, as seen in Deuteronomy 1:10; 10:22). (Ironside makes a clever connection between the dust and the "earthly" seed, and the stars in heaven and the "heavenly" seed, but Deuteronomy 1:10; 10:22 show this to be not true.)

A spiritual "seed" is also embraced within the Abrahamic promises. It is through his seed that all the nations will be blessed. Galatians 3:16 states clearly that the "seed" is Christ. Thus a key purpose for the national existence of Israel was to prepare the way for the birth of the Messiah. It is through Christ that the promise to Abraham has its full fruition. The nations will be blessed through faith as was their father Abraham. They are true "heirs according to the promise" (Galatians 3:29) because they are Abraham's true seed. "In Christ there is neither Jew nor Greek, for we are all one in Christ" (Galatians 3:28). Paul concludes the Galatian letter by addressing the "true seed," the "heirs of the promise," as the "Israel of God" (Galatians 6:16). The church of Christ is His new people; Christians are the sons of the promise, or of the "freewoman," as Paul allegorizes in Galatians 4. The sons of the "bondwoman," that is the unbelieving natural children, have been cast out (Galatians 4:30).

Israel Restored Forever

Israel is "restored" as a Messianic nation. The next several chapters will develop key elements of that restoration. It will be shown that the re-unification of "Israel and Judah" has been accomplished by the inclusion of Gentiles into the "new Israel of God." While the Gentile prophecies do not achieve the absolute New Testament concept of Jewish-Gentile equality, there are strong indications that the Gentiles are included *within Israel itself.* The fact that the church was no complete "mystery" is proven by the New Testament application of "Gentile" prophecies to the church. Jesus is now sitting on the promised "throne of David," drawing all nations to Himself, and the New Covenant promised to the "house of Israel" is now in effect.

The church itself, however, is actually only a glorious *phase* in God's plan of redemption. The ultimate restoration of Israel, for which the saints of both the Old and New Testaments await, is the consummation of the ages–the manifestation of Christ's eternal kingdom at His return. Several other chapters are devoted later to this grand theme as a demonstration that the Golden Age prophesied in the Old Testament and later magnificently portrayed in the book of Revelation is *eternal*, not millennial.

Rapture Woe #6

There are no land promises to Abraham that must yet be fulfilled. "Solomon ruled over all the kingdoms from the River to the land of the Philistines and to the border of Egypt ..." (I Kings 4:21). In fact, he had dominion over "everything west of the River" (I Kings 4:24).

4

LIVING UNDER THE
NEW COVENANT

An important act of restoration that the Messiah would accomplish for Israel was the establishment of a New Covenant with Israel. This promise, due to its precise "House of Israel" terminology in Jeremiah 31 and its pointed application in Hebrews to the New Testament church, becomes a major battleground concerning the dispensational position. Because of the importance this particular ramification carries regarding the entire futuristic view of later restoration, special emphasis must be placed upon establishing that Israel's New Covenant is now in effect. This definitely proves that the present church age is in fulfillment of Israel's promised restoration and Messianic Kingdom. The application of the New Covenant promise in Jeremiah 31 to the church in Hebrews 8-10 is a strong indication that there is something awry in the Rapture System's understanding of Israel's hope.

The Prophetic Promise of a New Covenant

The classic New Covenant passage is found in Jeremiah 31:31-34.

> "The time is coming," declares the LORD, "when I will make a new covenant with the house of Israel and with the house of Judah. It will not be like the covenant I made with their forefathers when I took them by the hand to lead them out of Egypt, because they broke my covenant, though I was a husband to them," declares the LORD. "This is the covenant I will make with the house of Israel after that time," declares the LORD. "I will put my law in their minds and write it on their hearts. I will be their God, and they will be my people. No longer will a man teach his neighbor, or a man his brother, saying,

'Know the LORD,' because they will all know me, from the least of them to the greatest," declares the LORD. "For I will forgive their wickedness and will remember their sins no more."

This New Covenant is closely connected with the concept of Israel's multiplication and blessing (Jeremiah 31:27-28), with the endurance of Israel as a "nation forever" (31:36), and with a re-alignment of Jerusalem's boundaries (31:38-40). Earlier in the chapter are the promises of restoration from "captivity" (31:4-14) and a likely reference to the Messiah's unique birth (the "new thing" in 31:22).

There are numerous other passages that provide useful parallels to Jeremiah 31. Jeremiah 3:16 speaks of the day when the ark of the covenant of the Lord will no longer be thought of. A New Covenant is clearly implied. Connected with this is the gathering of Gentiles to Jerusalem (3:17), and the re-unification of Israel and Judah (3:18), with the latter theme being implicit in Jeremiah 31. Both Jeremiah 32:40 and 50:5 promise an "everlasting covenant" that is to be equated with the New Covenant. Jeremiah 32:39 states, "And I will give them one heart and one way," (see 31:33), while Jeremiah 50:20 describes the sinlessness of restored Israel (see 31: 34).

Both Ezekiel 34:25 and 37:26 contain the pledge of a "covenant of peace" that is explicitly identified with the "everlasting covenant" (Ezekiel 37:26). Connected with this "covenant of peace" is the reign of the Messianic "David," the "one shepherd" over restored Israel (Ezekiel 34:23; 37:24). Promised also is God's dwelling in the midst of Israel forever (37: 26-28), while the ultimate result envisioned from this covenant is "Paradise itself" being restored (34:25-29; see also Hosea 2:18-20).

The fact that the New Covenant embraces such a rich variety of promises makes its application in the New Testament of major prophetic significance. The author of Hebrews 8 offers an indispensable guideline to interpreting restoration/Kingdom prophecy in his application of Jeremiah 31:31-34 to the New Testament church.

The Application Made In Hebrews 8

The main thrust of the book of Hebrews is that through Christ, the Christian economy is so much "better" than the Old Testament institutions. Christ is "better" than the angels (1:4-2:10), "better" than Moses (3:3-6), "better" than the Levitical priesthood (7:11), "better" than the Law (7:18-19), and is the mediator of a "better" covenant (8:6) through a "better" sacrifice (9:24-26). In the context of this entire argument, the writer of Hebrews quotes Jeremiah 31:31-34 (Hebrews 8:8-12). If his citation is to have any logical significance at all, it must be the declaration that the "better covenant" which Christ has enacted on "better promises" (8:6) is in fact the New Covenant which was promised to "the house of Israel" and "the house of Judah."

Dispensationalists, however, cannot make such an admission. Regarding the recipients of the New Covenant, Bernard Ramm explains,

> The strict literalists insist that this means Israel and Judah and not the Church for if it meant the Church we would have an unequivocal instance in which Israel is spoken to when the Church is meant and the essential distinction between Israel and the Church would be obliterated (*Protestant Biblical Interpretation*, p. 264).

The Rapture System will go to any extreme to preserve its imagined Israel-church distinction, as the following treatment of Hebrews 8 demonstrates.

The Dispensational Approach to the Problem

The dispensational scholar recognizes that he is in serious trouble when faced with the problem of exegesis presented by Hebrews 8. John F. Walvoord describes it as "the only passage which provides any difficulty to the premillennial view" (*The Millennial Kingdom*, pp. 215-16). This is wishful thinking, but it demonstrates the significance of this New Testament passage.

Walvoord discusses the various interpretations of the quotation in Hebrews, discarding the postmillennial view and labeling the amillennial view ("that the church is the true Israel") as "the most extreme of five possible views" (*Israel In Prophecy*, pp. 53-55). He is left with three possible dispensational views: (1) The New Covenant concerns Israel and Israel alone. This view was John Darby's and necessitates that Hebrews was not written to the church! (2) The New Covenant has a *twofold application* to the church in the present age and to Israel in the future millennial age (Scofield). (3) There are in fact *two* New Covenants, one for Israel to be fulfilled in the future; one for the church to be fulfilled in the present age; both founded upon the sacrifice of Christ (Lewis S. Chafer and others). Walvoord himself prefers the third approach, but admits that "there are problems that remain in the pre-millennial understanding of this passage" (*Israel In Prophecy*, p. 54).

The extent to which dispensationalists are blinded by their view regarding Israel is remarkable. H. A. Ironside states, "The New Covenant will some day be confirmed to Israel and Judah." Upon describing the internal aspects of the New Covenant, he adds, "This is already true of the believers in the Lord Jesus Christ" (*The Lamp of Prophecy*, p. 78). Richard DeHaan makes an equally striking remark: "Even as only a renewed people today enter the kingdom of God in the Church, so in the millennial age, the Jewish nation to whom the kingdom will be given be a new nation spiritually ...." (*Israel and the Nations*, pp. 62-63) Finally, C. I. Scofield makes the following statement:

> The New Covenant secures the personal revelation of the Lord to every believer; the complete oblivion of sins; rests upon an accomplished redemption; and secures the perpetuity, future conversion, and blessing of Israel (*The Scofield Reference Bible*, p. 1297).

Adherents to the Rapture System are united in their efforts to locate a future fulfillment of some kind for the New Covenant upon which the church was established.

The arguments upon which dispensationalists base their efforts are slim indeed. There are three basic lines of reasoning presented, the first two of which are merely dogmatic presuppositions, the third of which is a vain attempt at "splitting hairs."

(1) Regarding the promise of a New Covenant, J. Dwight Pentecost states, "The New Testament makes it clear that this promise is to be fulfilled only by the conversion of the nation at the second advent of Christ" (*Things to Come*, p. 534). He offers support for this "clear" teaching, however, with only one passage–Romans 11:26-27. Viewing this passage itself as supporting a future restoration, however, is possible only by ignoring the entire argument Paul presents in Romans 9-11.

(2) Another argument given is that the view of a fulfillment in the church fails to provide "any literal fulfillment of the covenant with Israel" (Walvoord, *The Millennial Kingdom*, p. 219). Again, this proposition

merely begs the question. If the New Testament views it as a "literal ful-fillment," what excuse is there to view it otherwise? The internal nature of the covenant Jeremiah describes is an exact picture of the relationship which the church enjoys with the Lord. G. Campbell Morgan states, "This is an exact description of the covenant under which Christian people live" (noted by William E. Cox, *Biblical Studies in Final Things*, p. 11). Oswald T. Allis exclaims, "It would be hard to find a clearer reference to the gospel age in the Old Testament than in these verses in Jeremiah; and the writer of Hebrews obviously appeals to it as such" (O. T. Allis, *Prophecy and the Church*, p. 154). (Aren't the initials "O. T." great for an Old Testament scholar?)

(3) The only argument that the Rapture System can muster on the basis of the text itself is a desperate attempt at "hair splitting." Wal-voord feebly tries to argue that the writer of Hebrews "does not say that Jeremiah's covenant is in effect now .... nowhere in the New Testament is the church specifically put under the detailed provisions of the covenant of Jeremiah" (*Israel in Prophecy*, p. 55). His amazing conclusion is, "The new covenant in force in the present age is not claimed to fulfill the new covenant with Israel at all" (Walvoord, *The Millennial Kingdom*, p. 217). Is that what the original recipients of the book of Hebrews would have understood? Hardly. Is this what Rapturists mean by following the "plain sense" of Scripture? The dispensational claim here needs careful scrutiny in light of the terminology found in Hebrews 8-10.

The Argument Against Dispensationalism from Hebrews 8-10

The overwhelming evidence found in Hebrews 8-10 offers as the only possible conclusion the fact that "Israel's" New Covenant is already in force. William E. Cox states, "The new covenant is already a reality as ev-idenced by the use of the present tense and the past tense in verse 6, 'But now *hath* he *obtained* . . . he *is* the mediator of a better covenant, which *hath been* enacted ....'" (*Biblical Studies in Final Things*, p. 9). Hebrews 10, dealing again with Jeremiah 31, further clarifies it. "Because by one sacri-fice he has made perfect forever those who are being made holy" (10:14). "Therefore, brothers, since we have confidence to enter the Most Holy Place by the blood of Jesus, by a new and living way opened for us through the curtain, that is, his body ...." (10:19-20). There is no indication that the new covenant is not yet in effect. Quite the opposite is true.

There needs to be a distinction made between the *offer* and the *acceptance* of Jeremiah's New Covenant. One of the characteristics of this covenant is that all its recipients would "know the Lord." The verb YADA' often indicates personal, experiential knowledge, not just intellectual assent. It would not be a knowledge dependent upon the mediation of priests and prophets, but access to God would be bold and confident (Ephesians 3:12). All would "know the Lord" since knowing would not be a *command* to those who were *under* the covenant, but rather it would be a necessary *condition* for *entrance* into that covenant relationship. The New Covenant was offered "once for all" at Calvary, but its acceptance is a gradual occurrence, since it is an individual, personal relationship into which believers enter. C. W. E. Naegelsbach says,

> If we should designate the day of the crucifixion as on the part of God the moment when He entered into the New Covenant relation, yet on the part of mankind there would then be no corresponding date of acceptance (*Jeremiah*, Lange's *Commentary*, p. 275).

The *offer* has already been made, and there is no Scriptural indication that a *later* offer will be made some day to national Israel. The fact that many refuse acceptance into the New Covenant does not negate the fact that it is *in force today*.

No Rapturist scenario can provide a better fulfillment of the New Covenant than Christ has *already* performed. He has "entered the holy place once for all, having obtained eternal redemption" through "His own blood" (Hebrews 9:12). Since the institutions upon earth are mere "copies and shadows of the heavenly things" (8:5; 9:28), the "better" covenant was mediated *in heaven itself.* "For Christ did not enter a holy place made with hands, a mere copy of the true one, but heaven itself, now to appear in the presence of God for us" (9:24). No greater fulfillment can be envisioned. Christ's incarnation and sacrificial death is described as "the consummation" (9:26). "For by one offering He has perfected for all time those who are sanctified" (10:14).

If the "second" covenant is *not* the New Covenant, then the writer of Hebrews has produced an outrageous misrepresentation. It is the *second* covenant by which Christians are sanctified (10:9-10), and there is no mention of a *third*. Dispensationalists have manufactured a *second* "New Covenant" that is an impossibility in light of the argument in Hebrews.

The passage in Hebrews 10:15-23 is conclusive in demonstrating that "Israel's" New Covenant is in effect with the church.

> The Holy Spirit also testifies to us about this. First he says: "This is the covenant I will make with them after that time, says the Lord. I will put my laws in their hearts, and I will write them on their minds." Then he adds: "Their sins and lawless acts I will remember no more." And where these have been forgiven, there is no longer any sacrifice for sin. Therefore, brothers, since we have confidence to enter the Most Holy Place by the blood of Jesus, by a new and living way opened for us through the curtain, that is, his body, and since we have a great priest over the house of God, let us draw near to God with a sincere heart in full assurance of faith, having our hearts sprinkled to cleanse us from a guilty conscience and having our bodies washed with pure water. Let us hold unswervingly to the hope we profess, for he who promised is faithful.

Hebrews clearly states that Jeremiah's New Covenant promise "testifies to us" as the revelation of the Holy Spirit (10:15). The passage speaks to the church. The writer comments upon the citation by concluding, "And where these have been forgiven, there is no longer any sacrifice for sin" (10:18). The argument is air-tight.

As noted in the chapter "The Millenial Maze," the new breed of Rapturists known as Progressive Dispensationalists pretty much concedes the point made in this chapter, to the great dismay of the classic dispensationalists (Walvoord, Lindsey, LaHaye, Ryrie, Ice, etc.). Dispensationalism has indeed become "a house divided." The Progressive Dispensationalists still believe in many of the basic dispensational doctrines, but their admission that the church fulfills many Old Testament prophecies is a dagger in the heart of the Postponement Theory, which is the rationale for many of the unlikely jumps and gaps that they build into their interpretations of prophecy. It will be interesting to see what eventually becomes of the Progressive Dispensationalists.

If the promise under "Israel's" New Covenant is actually realized in the church age, as Hebrews explicitly teaches, then the New Covenant itself must already be a reality. To separate the New Covenant from its aspects or blessings is to render Scripture unintelligible. The Jews will only realize their New Covenant relationship to God as they enjoy it in the body of Christ.

5

NO VACANCY
ON DAVID'S THRONE

A key aspect of Israel's future Kingdom hope is the eternal reign of the Messiah. This reign is figuratively described as being on "the throne of David." David, often pictured as Israel's ideal ruler, is himself superseded by One whose reign will be perfect and eternal.

As in the case of the New Covenant, the issue vital to the correct understanding of Israel's glorious restoration revolves around the time element involved. If Israel's restoration still awaits the future, then Christ's present heavenly reign cannot be the promised "Davidic" reign. However, if the Scriptures view Christ as presently occupying "David's throne," then it must be admitted that Israel's restoration is a reality in the church age. Its promised Kingdom is in the realm of the "already."

The Promise of a Future "Throne of David"

The promise of the restoration of "Davidic" rule was a major prophetic theme. This promise is generally designated as the Davidic Covenant. The promise set forth in II Samuel 7 was that one of David's own descendants would be raised up to reign forever upon the throne of the kingdom. The prophetic development of this promise makes it clear that it is to be fulfilled ultimately in the Messiah himself.

Isaiah explicitly describes the Messiah's eternal reign as being "on the throne of David" (Isaiah 9:7). Elsewhere he describes Him as being a judge sitting in the "tent of David" (Isaiah 16:5). The promise Isaiah extends of a future "leader and commander" (Isaiah 55:4) is in accordance to "the faithful mercies shown to David" (Isaiah 55:3), i.e., in accordance to the promise of a future Davidic ruler. The Messiah's Davidic ancestry is further implied by the expressions "stem of Jesse" (Isaiah 11:1) and "root of Jesse" (Isaiah 11:10).

The prophets Jeremiah and Ezekiel continue the Davidic theme. The Messiah is described by Jeremiah as a "righteous Branch of David" (Jeremiah 33:15; 23:5). Jeremiah says, "A King who will reign wisely and do what is just and right in the land" (Jeremiah 23:5b). In His days, "Judah will be saved" (Jeremiah 23:6). Both Jeremiah and Ezekiel describe the Messiah with the rather startling title "David their king" (Jeremiah 30:9; Ezekiel 34:23-24; 37:24-25; also Hosea 3:5). This expression is naturally taken by most to be a figurative designation of the Messiah Himself.

Many dispensationalists, however, due to their insistence upon extreme literalism when it comes to matters pertaining to Israel, suggest that *David himself will be resurrected* to share with Christ in the Millennial reign. David will supposedly be a "prince" ruling under Christ, the "king." This prince-king distinction, however, clearly breaks down in Ezekiel 37: 24-25, where "David" is called *both* king *and* prince. He also is the "one shepherd" set over the people (Ezekiel 34:23). But there is no hint here of two separate rulers. If there will be just "one shepherd" appointed over the Kingdom saints, I know who gets my vote. Sorry, David.

The Rapturist view is plagued with absurdities at this point. Either (1) Christ and David will squeeze together on the same "literal" throne or (2) there will be *two* literal thrones: "a throne of David" for David and a "throne of David" for Christ, or (3) Christ and David will have to take turns. Such unlikely possibilities only present themselves as live options as a result of what Rapturists have deemed "normal and natural exegesis."

One further point needs consideration before the New Testament evidence itself is examined. The prophets repeatedly viewed the future "David" in connection with the conversion of the Gentiles. Isaiah says,

"In that day the Root of Jesse will stand as a banner for the peoples; the nations will rally to him, and his place of rest will be glorious" (Isaiah 11:10). He offers this similar description of the Messianic king:

> Behold, I have made him a witness to the peoples, a leader and commander for the peoples. Behold, you will call a nation you do not

know, and a nation which knows you not will run to you (Isaiah 55: 4-5a).

Paul cites Isaiah 65:1, a parallel passage to 55:5a, in reference to the conversion of Gentiles in the church age (Romans 10:20).

In another Messianic prophecy, Jeremiah predicts that the seed of "David" will be multiplied as the "host of heaven" and the "sand of the sea" (Jeremiah 33:22). This undoubtedly refers to the incorporation of Gentiles into the Messianic kingdom. With these remarks in mind, we can better appreciate the New Testament evidence.

David's Throne and the New Testament

The united testimony of the New Testament writers is that Christ is presently seated on the Messianic "throne of David." This fact will be demonstrated in the following studies: (1) David's throne and Christ's present reign; (2) David's throne and Christ's resurrection; (3) David's throne and Christ's royal priesthood; and (4) David's throne and the argument from Acts 15.

David's Throne and Christ's Present Reign

According to ample New Testament testimony, Christ is now seated at the right hand of God (Acts 2:33; Romans 8:34; Ephesians 1:20; Colossians 3:1; I Peter 3:22). John F. Walvoord, former president of Dallas Theological Seminary, is representative of the Rapture System in his contention that there is no justification for identifying David's throne with the Father's throne. He claims,

> Of the 59 references to David in the New Testament, there is not one connecting the Davidic throne with the present session of Christ. Such an inference could be established only by spiritualizing many prophecies both in the Old and New Testaments. (*Israel in Prophecy*, p. 96)

The above is a startling statement, one that cannot stand under any form of objective scrutiny. To test the validity of the dispensational claim, we need to determine the kind of throne that would fulfill the intent of prophecy. James Bales comments,

As far as the writer knows, no one maintains that the literal, physical chair or throne on which David sat is preserved somewhere and will be sat on by Christ. This is no more believed than that the statement about Moses' seat (Matt. 23:1, 2) meant the very seat on which Moses had sat. If it did, it was a mighty big seat, for the scribes and Pharisees sat in it; or else they had to do a lot of rotation in order for all to sit a little while in it. (*New Testament Interpretation of Kingdom Prophecies*, p. 12)

Walvoord himself states, "By the term 'throne' it is clear that no reference is made to a material throne but rather to the dignity and power which was sovereign and supreme in David as king." Such words are remarkable in light of Walvoord's view of the present reign of Christ:

The throne in heaven on which Christ is now seated is obviously one of supreme honor, glory, victory, power, and authority. No power on earth or in heaven could possibly have a higher position nor could there be one of more honor and privilege than that which the Lord Jesus Christ now possesses.[1]

Walvoord contends however, that the throne of David does not fit the above description, for it was not one of infinite power and authority. Such a position is logically untenable. Surely Walvoord would not disagree with the view that Messianic reign will be greater in all respects than that which David enjoyed. Yet he maintains that when Christ comes with power to "establish" His glorious kingdom, he will actually take a step *down* in position! The Davidic reign, so goes Walvoord's logic, will not begin to compare with that which He now enjoys. How can it be that His "hastily-contrived banishment in heaven" will surpass in majesty and power the earthly reign to which all the glorious Old Testament prophecies supposedly point?

Dispensationalists display the same lack of understanding that characterized the Pharisees of Jesus' day. Since the Jewish leaders agreed that the Messiah was to be David's "Son," Jesus asked,

"What do you think about the Christ? Whose son is he?" "The son of David," they replied. He said to them, "How is it then that David, speaking by the Spirit, calls him 'Lord'? For he says, 'The Lord said to my Lord: "Sit at my right hand until I put your enemies under your feet."' If then David calls him 'Lord,' how can he be his

---

[1] John F. Walvoord, "The Present Universal Lordship of Christ," *Bibliotheca Sacra* (April, 1964), p. 101.

son?" No one could say a word in reply, and from that day on no one dared to ask him any more questions.

The Pharisees had no answer, since they did not realize that the Messiah would not be a mere political, earthly ruler as David had been, but rather the divine, universal savior-king whose reign would be "far above all rule and authority, power and dominion, and every title that can be given, not only in the present age but also in the one to come" (Ephesians 1:21). David's typical reign is greatly surpassed by the antitype–Christ's glorious reign.

It is true that presently Christ is not *visibly* exerting His full authority over man. He will do so at the final consummation of the Kingdom. This change in the manifestation of power, however, in no way necessitates or ever suggests a change in thrones. It is even more incredible to maintain that in Christ's "hour of triumph in which history will come to its close, and the power, sovereignty, and majesty of Christ will be obvious to every creature."[2] He will assume a *lesser throne* than that which He now occupies.

David's Throne and Christ's Resurrection

Charles H. Stephens minimizes Christ's present reign with a dispensational shrug when he states, "David's throne is vacant. The king is 'exiled' in heaven."[3] The clear teaching of the New Testament, however, is that Christ's ascension into heaven was an act of *coronation*, not a banishment into "exile," and that in His resurrection and subsequent ascension, He fulfilled the promises regarding the throne of David. Acts 2:29-36 and Acts 13:32-37 offer proof that the resurrection, which ushered in the present reign of Christ in heaven, was in fulfillment of the promises to David. After citing David's prophecy in Psalm 16:8-11, Peter explained,

> But he was a prophet and knew that God had promised him on oath that he would place one of his descendants on his throne. Seeing what was ahead, he spoke of the resurrection of the Christ, that he was not abandoned to the grave, nor did his body see decay. (Acts 2:30-31)

---

[2] John F. Walvoord, "The Present Universal Lordship of Christ," p. 106

[3] Charles H. Stephens, "The Church of Christ and the Kingdom of Christ In Contrast," in *Prophecy in the Seventies*, Charles Feinberg, editor (Chicago: Moody Press, 1971), p. 102.

As a result of His resurrection, Christ was exalted to the right hand of God (Acts 2:33), and Peter concluded his argument by proclaiming Christ's God-given *Lordship over all the house of Israel* (Acts 2:36). As Peter uttered the very words, Christ's reign over the house of Israel was a reality.

Paul utilized the same line of reasoning as he preached in the synagogue at Antioch of Pisidia. He declared that God fulfilled His promise made to the fathers "in that He raised up Jesus" (Acts 13:32-33). This promise was also called "the sure mercies of David" (Isaiah 55:3; Acts 13: 34). The resurrection is seen to be that occasion of which Psalm 2 speaks: "Thou art My Son, today I have begotten thee" (Psalm 2:7 *King James Version*; Acts 13:33). Following the crucifixion, Christ "was declared with power to be the Son of God by his resurrection from the dead" (Romans 1:4).

After Christ's resurrection, He was exalted to God's right hand as a "Prince and a Savior" (Acts 5:31; the Greek ARCHEGOS is commonly translated "chief leader, prince"; see Acts 3:15). If Christ is now ruling as "Prince," what Scriptural basis is there for Christ's assuming a *later* office of "Prince"? The only basis is a misguided literalism which refuses to take the New Testament *literally* in its inspired interpretation of Old Testament prophecy.

It is strange that, if the promise to David would not be fulfilled until many centuries later, Peter cited it on Pentecost. If Christ's resurrection was *not* in fulfillment of the promise to David, then Peter seems to have been thousands of years off the subject. Even stranger is that nowhere in the New Testament is a future reign on David's throne promised to Christ subsequent to His resurrection. Christ's claims to the throne resulted from His resurrection from the dead.

Walvoord himself agrees that Christ's present authority stems from His resurrection (see Ephesians 1:20-22) ("The Present Universal Lordship of Christ," p. 103). The New Testament maintains that this present authority is "over all the House of Israel" and is in fulfillment of the promises to David.

David's Throne and Christ's Royal Priesthood

The messianic king would be not only a ruler, but also a suffering savior (see Psalm 22; Isaiah 53). The New Testament portrays Christ's suffering and exaltation as a connected, consecutive sequence of events. It was after "he had made purification of his sins" that "He sat down at the right hand of the Majesty on high" (Hebrews 1:3; see also Hebrews 10:12; 12:2; Luke 24:26). Only after He overcame "the prince of this world" could He claim His true kingship (John 12:31; 16:11; also Hebrews 2:14; I John 3:5, 8). Additionally, it was through Christ's suffering, the book of Hebrews explains, that He was given the honor of "high priest according to the order of Melchizedek" (Hebrews 5:1-10).

The climax of the Old Testament's Messianic revelation is the knowledge that the Messiah would be "a priest on His throne" (Zechariah 6: 12; see also Psalm 110, the kingly "order of Melchizedek"). This combination forbidden by Jewish law would become a reality in the Messiah. It is being fulfilled in the *present* reign of Christ. Paul describes Jesus as He "who is at the right hand of God, who also intercedes for us" (Romans 8:34). As king He is also engaged in the priestly function of intercession. The writer of Hebrews summarized thus,

> The point of what we are saying is this: We do have such a high priest, who sat down at the right hand of the throne of the Majesty in heaven, and who serves in the sanctuary, the true tabernacle set up by the Lord, not by man. (Hebrews 8:1-2)

Christ's priestly office is clearly shown to be a reality now in the church age (see also Hebrews 7:24-28). He is also without doubt presently "a priest on His throne." There is no other possible conclusion to draw but that Christ's present reign fulfills the promise of Zechariah 6:12 and other passages.

There is no Scriptural basis for maintaining that Christ's priesthood and kingship are two different offices that have been separated in time now by nearly two thousand years. The New Testament indicates rather that through both the suffering and exaltation of the Son of David, God's promises to Israel were fulfilled. Just as Christ ministers in the "true tabernacle, which the Lord pitched," so He reigns on the "true throne," the intended Messianic throne to which He was elevated after He had "accomplished the work God gave Him to do" (John 17:4, paraphrase).

David's Throne and the Argument from Acts 15

Regarding Acts 15:13-18 Scofield remarked, "Dispensationally, this is the most important passage in the N.T." (*Scofield Reference Bible*, p. 1169). The importance of this passage, however, is not in its *support* of dispensationalism, but rather in its refutation of that system. Walvoord at least recognizes its dangers when he states,

> About the only reference that can be construed as having any connection with the identification of David's kingdom reign and the present session of Christ is that found in Acts 15:14-17 (*The Millennial Kingdom*, pp. 203-4).

The significance of Acts 15:13-18 is that it is one of the clearest indications that the promises to David are being fulfilled in the church age. The discussion found in Acts 15 concerns the Jerusalem conference. The topic at hand was the issue of whether or not circumcision was essential for Gentiles converted to Christianity. The decision arrived at was that it was not, and the conclusive argument was presented by James, the brother of Jesus. He said,

> Brothers, listen to me. Simon has described to us how God at first showed his concern by taking from the Gentiles a people for himself. The words of the prophets are in agreement with this, as it is written: "After this I will return and rebuild David's fallen tent. Its ruins I will rebuild, and I will restore it, that the remnant of men may seek the Lord, and all the Gentiles who bear my name, says the Lord, who does these things that have been known for ages." (Acts 15:13-18, citing Amos 9:11-12)

The natural interpretation of James' usage of Amos 9:11-12 is that, regarding the events under investigation at the conference, James saw in them the fulfillment of the "rebuilding of David's tabernacle" and the conversion of the Gentiles. With James' interpretation of Amos' prophecy, Peter, Paul and the others apparently concurred, for it signaled the end of the discussion.

The Rapturists deny this entire premise. They view that the events of the early church had nothing to do with Amos' prophecy, but that the fulfillment awaits the Millennium. According to their spokesmen, only when the prophecy is "spiritualized" can it be seen to be applied to the present age.[4]

The threads upon which the dispensational argument hangs are three separate words or phrases: (1) "agrees;" (2) "after there things;" and (3) "I will return."

(1) Willard M. Aldrich points out that Acts 15:15 is the only New Testament usage of the word "agree" in introducing a prophetic quotation (p. 319). This is an important point in his argument, for he views the inclusion of Gentiles into the church as not "fulfilling" Amos' words, but only "agreeing" with them. "*Harmony* not *identity* is indicated," and James' words merely mean, "If God has it in His heart to save them in the future, then His present work is agreeable to such a heart attitude" (p. 319).

This special significance for the word "agree," however, has no positive support. It is purely a matter of speculation, and should be rejected in light of the fact that not only is the future coming of Christ not in focus, but it has absolutely nothing whatsoever to do with the subject under debate. The term "agrees" may signify a corporate consent since the plural "prophets" is used. The quotation is actually a paraphrase and probably incorporates the terminology of other passages (e.g. Isaiah 45:21; Jeremiah 12:15; Joel 2:28).

(2) Aldrich deems it significant that the phrase "after these things" is not part of Amos' original quotation. James' purpose in altering the original was, in his estimation, "for the very purpose of making it clear that the Old Testament prophecy is not fulfilled in the Gentile inclusion in the church" (p. 321). The words "these things," then, are supposed to have reference to God's present work among the Gentiles. David's tent will be restored, then, *after* the Church Age.

In response it must be noted that "in that day" (the original expression in Amos 9), "after these things," and "in the latter days" are all Messianic formulas which defy a precise attempt at determining a specific frame of reference. This is especially true of "in that day" (e.g., Isaiah 4:2). It is likely that James' introductory formula has no special significance.

---

[4] Willard M. Aldrich, "The Interpretation of Acts 15:13-18," *Bibliotheca Sacra* 111 (October, 1954), p. 317. This is one of the more detailed dispensational attempts to try to deal with this "problem" text.

Joel's prophecy cited by Peter at Pentecost (most certainly a reference to the Church Age) began with "after this" in the Hebrew, but is introduced by Peter with "and it shall be in the last days" (Acts 2:17). How precarious to base the weight of an argument upon such a minor point, especially in the face of the circumstances in Acts 15.

Aldrich's argument that explains the switch from "in that day" to "after these things" is erroneous. He claims that the frame of reference in Amos 9:9-10 is the "Great Tribulation," while in Acts 15 it is the present Church Age. The Millennium is immediately connected to the supposed tribulation context of Amos by "in that day," while it is removed from the present calling of the Gentiles in Acts by the more remote expression "after these things" (pp. 321-22).

Amos 9:9-10, however, has nothing to do with a future tribulation for Israel, but rather, in fitting with the entire message of Amos, it refers to the process of dispersion and preservation accompanying the Assyrian captivity. The audience to which the eighth-century prophet spoke was about to go into exile. With respect to the events and results of the captivity, one could view the New Testament restoration as being "in that day," or as James paraphrases, "after these things."

(3) Walvoord views the phrase "I will return" as an apparent reference to the Second Coming of Christ. "That it could not refer either to the incarnation or to the coming of the Spirit at Pentecost is evident in that neither is a 'return'" (*The Millennial Kingdom*, p. 206). Aldrich cites the Greek lexicographer Thayer in support of his own views that "I will return" refers to the personal return of Christ (p. 322). He misrepresents Thayer, however, in that Thayer is *not* referring to the Second Coming (as is Aldrich) but rather to the *first* advent. Thayer says that "God in the Messiah's advent returns to his people, whom he is conceived of as having previously abandoned" (Joseph Henry Thayer, *A Greek-English Lexicon of the New Testament*, p. 42). In no way can the Second Coming be spoken of as being in connection with an "abandonment." Thayer is speaking of Christ's first coming.

While it is not absolutely clear from which prophecy James is lifting the phrase "I will return," there are several possibilities. The key point is that this "return" is in connection with the calamity of the Assyrian, and later Babylonian, captivity, and therefore is a reference to Christ's first advent. The most likely passage from which James may have borrowed is Jeremiah 12:15, where the Hebrew literally says that "after I have up-rooted them, I will return (or "turn"–SHUB) and I will have compassion upon them." This divine visitation is viewed as a "turning" or "returning" with respect to God's previous visitation in judgement, not with respect to the first coming of Christ. This divine reversal is also expressed, e.g., in Jeremiah 33:26. "But I will restore their fortunes and will have mercy on them." The prophecy of restoration in Hosea 11:9-11 includes the promise, "I will not return (SHUB) to destroy Ephraim" (Hosea 11:9). The scattering as a result of the Babylonian captivity (Zechariah 7:14) is followed by the restoration promise in which God would "return to Zion" (Zechariah 8:3). Similarly, the seventy years of captivity (Zechariah 1: 12), will be followed by a return of God's favor. The Lord promises, "I will return to Jerusalem with mercy, and there my house will be rebuilt" (Zechariah 1:16). A proper understanding of the above passages leads one to conclude that God's "return" is in fact a term used in Old Testament prophecy to refer to the first advent. James obviously applies the phrase accordingly in Acts 15.

Upon examination of the dispensational arguments, there is no solid basis for viewing James' argument in other than its most obvious sense. He is viewing the inclusion of Gentiles into the church as the fulfillment of Amos' prophecy in particular, and of the united testimony of the Old Testament prophets in general. Taking it in its logical connection, James' argument agrees with the abundant New Testament evidence already cited that the Davidic Covenant has been and is being fulfilled in Christ's resurrection, ascension, enthronement and present heavenly reign.

Again, the recent Progressive Dispensationalism movement concedes the point here, putting them at odds with the more traditional (and consistent) Rapture System. With their admission, however, the linchpin Postponement Theory goes out the window, creating problems for many of their postponement-driven interpretations. It is a serious dilemma that must eventually be addressed by these reformers.

If the New Testament is taken as the guide, however, there can be no mistake regarding the fulfillment of this glorious prophetic theme, for its testimony indicates clearly that Christ's present Messianic reign fulfills the Davidic Covenant. The promise has nothing to do with a future, earthly, nationalistic, political arrangement like the one dispensational-ists envision.

There is currently "NO VACANCY" on David's throne. Christ Jesus, the promised Messianic King, reigns upon it right now.

Rapture Woe #7

The promised conversion of the Gentiles began its fulfillment in the first century efforts of the New Testament Christians. This was in fulfillment of the promises to David. No future Millennial Kingdom is needed for a fulfillment.

6

EGYPT MY PEOPLE

> In that day there will be a highway from Egypt to Assyria. The
> Assyrians will go to Egypt and the Egyptians to Assyria. The Egyp-
> tians and Assyrians will worship together. In that day Israel will
> be the third, along with Egypt and Assyria, a blessing on the earth.
> The LORD Almighty will bless them, saying, "Blessed be Egypt my
> people, Assyria my handiwork, and Israel my inheritance." (Isaiah
> 19:23-25)

One of the clear signals that the promised messianic king had arrived
would be the flocking of the nations ("Gentiles") unto him.

> Behold, I have made him a witness to the peoples, a leader and
> commander for the peoples. Behold, you will call a nation you do
> not know, and a nation which knows you not will run to you. (Isaiah
> 55:4-5a)

In the previous chapter it was demonstrated that Christ began his
"throne-of-David rule" when his lordship over the church commenced.
The Scriptures declare that when David's dynasty would re-emerge from
the ashes portrayed in the closing pages of the Old Testament record,
and the eternal "David" would sit on the throne forever, then all nations
would seek the Lord.

> I will return and rebuild David's fallen tent. Its ruins I will re-
> build, and I will restore it, that the remnant of men may seek the
> Lord, and all the Gentiles who bear my name, says the Lord, who
> does these things that have been known for ages." (Acts 15:13-18,
> citing Amos 9:11-12)

The theme of the conversion of the Gentiles in the messianic age,
then, is clearly linked to the fact that the messianic king would be their
leader.

The Gentiles and the Messianic Re-Unification

The re-unification envisioned by the prophets involves much more than the mere political merger of the Northern and Southern Kingdoms. Re-unification in its fullest sense depends upon the Messiah alone. This is clearly stated in Ezekiel 34 and 37. The scattered flock of Israel would be united under "one shepherd," even "David" (Ezekiel 34:23). The Lord promises,

> I will make them one nation in the land, on the mountains of Israel. There will be one king over all of them and they will never again be two nations or be divided into two kingdoms. They will no longer defile themselves with their idols and vile images or with any of their offenses, for I will save them from all their sinful backsliding, and I will cleanse them. They will be my people, and I will be their God. My servant David will be king over them, and they will all have one shepherd. (Ezekiel 37:22-24a)

The "one king" over them would be "David" (Ezekiel 37:24). The promise of re-unification is also implicit in Jeremiah's New Covenant prophecy. The New Covenant would be made both with the house of Israel and the house of Judah (Jeremiah 31:31).

The fulfillment of this re-unification promise is the New Testament church. This is to be expected since both the New Covenant and "David" promises have already been fulfilled by Christ. Re-unification is seen fulfilled by the *union* of Jews and Gentiles into the New Testament church (see e.g., Ephesians 2:15–"one new man").

Key to this New Testament application of a "nationalistic-sounding" promise is Paul's usage of certain prophecies of Hosea. One of Hosea's children was named Lo-ammi (meaning "not my people"), a designation of Israel's severed relationship to God (Hosea 1:9). Another was named Lo-Ruchamah, "not beloved." The promise of the restoration of Lo-ammi and Lo-Ruchamah, however, is then given:

> Yet the Israelites will be like the sand on the seashore, which cannot be measured or counted. In the place where it was said to them, "You are not my people," they will be called "sons of the living God." I will plant her for myself in the land; I will show my love to the one I called "Not my loved one." I will say to those called "Not my people," "You are my people"; and they will say, "You are my God." (Hosea 1:10; 2:23)

Note this crucial point. While the prophet Hosea uses this expression in reference to the apostate Northern Kingdom, the Apostle Paul cites this prophecy in reference to the *conversion of the Gentiles* (Romans 9:25-26). In the eyes of God, apparently, Israel had become like Gentiles, "Lo-ammi" (see also Am. 9:7–"Are you not as the sons of Ethiopia to Me, O sons of Israel?"). *Thus the fulfillment of Israel's re-unification with Judah is the union of Gentiles with Jews to form the New Testament church.*

In harmony with the theme of re-unification, much of Old Testament "restoration" prophecy involves the conversion of the Gentiles. Isaiah is especially concerned with this major prophetic theme. In the pages to follow we will outline the Old Testament's treatment of this theme. In the present treatment it is impossible to go into great depth in discussing each text. However, those who insist on extreme literalism here will find themselves coming to a very different conclusion from what the New Testament apostles seem to have arrived at.

We will survey the following topics: (1) the Gentiles journey to Israel; (2) the Gentiles join themselves to Israel; (3) the Gentiles subject themselves to Israel; (4) the Gentiles join in the worship of the God of Israel; (5) the Gentiles bring their wealth to Israel; and (6) the Gentiles greatly enlarge Israel. The benefits of such a study should become apparent.

The Gentiles Journey to Israel

The prophets paint the picture of a mass Gentile migration to Israel. Concerning the days when the ark of the covenant would no longer be remembered (Jeremiah 3:16), Jeremiah declares:

> At that time they will call Jerusalem The Throne of the LORD, and all nations will gather in Jerusalem to honor the name of the LORD. No longer will they follow the stubbornness of their evil hearts. (Jeremiah 3:17)

Isaiah prophecies that in the "last days," the mountain of the Lord will be established above all others and that "all the nations will stream to it" (Isaiah 2:2).

> Many peoples will come and say, "Come, let us go up to the mountain of the LORD, to the house of the God of Jacob. He will teach us his ways, so that we may walk in his paths." The law will go out from Zion, the word of the LORD from Jerusalem. (Isaiah 2:3)

It is not Israel itself which attracts the crowds, but Israel's "light," the "glory of the Lord" (Isaiah 61:1). The promise, then, is: "And nations will come to your light, and kings to the brightness of your rising" (Isaiah 60:3). This gathering is described as a return of Israel's "sons and daughters":

> Lift up your eyes and look about you: All assemble and come to you; your sons come from afar, and your daughters are carried on the arm. (Isaiah 60:4)

These "sons and daughters" are the result of God's summons to the nations:

> This is what the Sovereign LORD says: "See, I will beckon to the Gentiles, I will lift up my banner to the peoples; they will bring your sons in their arms and carry your daughters on their shoulders." (Isaiah 49:22)

Surely even the wildest millennial scene lurking in the minds of the dispensationalists would not feature a "literal" fulfillment here.

The Gentiles Join Themselves to Israel

It is important to realize, however, that not only do the Gentiles come *to* Israel, but also they join *with* Israel. Pictured in Zechariah is mutual or joint restoration:

> "Shout and be glad, O Daughter of Zion. For I am coming, and I will live among you," declares the LORD. "Many nations will be joined with the LORD in that day and will become my people. I will live among you and you will know that the LORD Almighty has sent me to you. The LORD will inherit Judah as his portion in the holy land and will again choose Jerusalem." (Zechariah 2:10-12)

God will dwell in the midst of "His people"–both Jews and Gentiles, as the passage indicates (see Romans 9:24-26; Ephesians 2:13-18).

The scene found in Isaiah 54 is that of Israel "enlarging her tent" and "spreading abroad to the right and the left" in order to "possess nations" (54:2-3). Thus Israel's "tent" includes both Jews and Gentiles. Similarly, in Amos 9, the rebuilding of David's "fallen hut" is connected with the possession of the "remnant of Edom" and "all the nations who are called by My name" (Amos 9:11-12). The Gentiles, as well as the Jews, would then be called by God's "name." Israel's "borders" would be greatly extended.

A remarkable passage is found in Jeremiah 12:14-17. The Lord is addressing Israel's wicked neighbors "who strike at the inheritance with which I have endowed My people Israel" (12:14a). Thus the word of the Lord promises, "Behold I am about to uproot them from their land and will uproot the house of Judah from among them" (12:15b). Following this threat is the hope of a Gentile "restoration":

> "But after I uproot them, I will again have compassion and will bring each of them back to his own inheritance and his own country. And if they learn well the ways of my people and swear by my name, saying, 'As surely as the LORD lives'–even as they once taught my people to swear by Baal–then they will be established among my people. But if any nation does not listen, I will completely uproot and destroy it," declares the LORD. (Jeremiah 12:15-17)

Several observations can be made concerning this restoration of Israel's neighbors: (1) This restoration would begin with the return of each nation to its *own* land. The policy of Persian kings which allowed the Jews to return was a blank check for all captive peoples. Thus this promise was historically fulfilled through the decree of Cyrus.

(2) Their conversion would take place in their own land, yet the would"learn the ways of God's people," to "swear by His name." Such a conversion under the *old* Jewish economy would involve participation in the ceremonies and festivals involving Jerusalem. No such concept is here implied. A turning to the Lord is involved, but not a turning to national Israel as such.

(3) The Lord promises that as a result of their conversion, "they will be built up in the midst of My people." The implications here are tremendous. It would be natural to hear the promise regarding Israel's neighbors that Israel would be built up in the midst of *them*, or that they would be built up *around her*, but here is the promise that these neighbors would one day be built up "in the midst of My people." The only possible interpretation is that they would be incorporated into Israel. They would remain in their own lands, but would be in the midst of God's people–a truly remarkable prophecy of the conversion of the Gentiles as witnessed in the pages of the New Testament.

(4) Failure to accept this opportunity would result in destruction for the nation. It is true that none of Israel's old neighbors are around any-more–e.g., the Philistines, the Moabites, and the Edomites–yet this threat may involve more than just national oblivion. Certainly the conversion spoken of involves individuals, and the threat of national punishment could be taken to include God's eternal condemnation upon all sinners. The spiritual decay of a Godless nation would end in physical destruction as well.

The Gentiles Subject Themselves to Israel

One of the striking themes of Isaiah's Gentile prophecies is that of Israel's subjection of Gentile nations. An unfortunate consequence of hyperliteral interpretation is that which is seen in the dispensationalists' Millennium. The picture they offer is one of Gentile servitude to Israel. Walvoord maintains that in the Millennium Israel will be exalted above the Gentiles, and cites no less than twenty-seven Scripture references supposed to prove the "lesser role" of Gentiles in the Millennium. While "the Gentiles will share many of the spiritual and economic blessings of the millennial reign of Christ," they will "occupy a subordinate role to Israel."

Pentecost suggests, "The nations which usurped authority over Israel in past ages find that downtrodden people exalted and themselves in sub-jection in their kingdom." And yet these are the same Gentiles, Pentecost asserts, of whom it is said, "Come, ye blessed of my Father, inherit the kingdom prepared for you from the foundation of the world" (Matthew 25:34). According to the dispensationalists, the Gentiles' inheritance is "blessed slavery." They were designed "from the foundation of the world" to be in political and economic subjection to Israel for a thousand years. (No wonder so many will "rebel" at the end of the Millennium.) It is an incredible picture that the dispensationalists paint, one not even hinted at throughout the entire New Testament.

Upon studying these prophecies in Isaiah it would be well to keep in mind the political background of Isaiah's words. Israel indeed is op-pressed by Assyria (by the time of the writing of these prophecies the Northern Kingdom has already fallen). Hezekiah in the South is forced to pay high tribute to Sennacherib, so much so that he is forced to cut off the gold from the doors and doorposts of the temple (II Kings 18: 14-16). The threat from other nations has been a continual thorn in the nation's side. It would be quite natural for Isaiah's glorious prophecies to be clothed in the language of the current political situation, just as they were often veiled in the language of the Old Testament religious economy (e.g., "grain offering," "priests and Levites," Isaiah 66:20-21; see also Jeremiah 33:18; Haggai 2:7-9; Zechariah 14:16). For the Gentile nations to be in total subjection to Israel would indeed be a "turning of captivity," a "reversal of fortunes."

Isaiah 14:1 predicts that strangers would *join Israel in their land* and "attach themselves to the house of Jacob." Verse 2 continues:

> Nations will take them and bring them to their own place. And the house of Israel will possess the nations as menservants and maidservants in the LORD's land. They will make captives of their captors and rule over their oppressors. (Isaiah 14:2)

The political background is stressed in verse 3 where the oppression at the hand of the king of Babylon is alluded to. The Lord would give rest from "pain and turmoil and harsh service" in which they had been enslaved. This amazing reversal of fortunes is also suggested in Isaiah 61: 5 where God promises, "And strangers will stand and pasture your flocks, and foreigners will be your farmers and your vinedressers." It is especially noted that even the foreign kings would serve them (60:10) and bow down to them (49:23). The shame of Israel would no longer exist:

> Kings will be your foster fathers, and their queens your nursing mothers. They will bow down before you with their faces to the ground; they will lick the dust at your feet. Then you will know that I am the LORD; those who hope in me will not be disappointed. (Isaiah 49:23)

Certainly a strictly literal interpretation of this, applied to millennial saints, totally contradicts any concept of salvation that the Bible presents.

Two final passages shed light upon a correct understanding of Gentile submission to Israel. The first is Isaiah 45:14. Pictured here is submission to Israel because of her relationship to God.

> This is what the LORD says: "The products of Egypt and the merchandise of Cush, and those tall Sabeans—they will come over to

you and will be yours; they will trudge behind you, coming over to you in chains. They will bow down before you and plead with you, saying, 'Surely God is with you, and there is no other; there is no other god.'"

The second passage is Isaiah 49:7, a description of the Messianic "Servant of the Lord":

This is what the LORD says–the Redeemer and Holy One of Israel–to him who was despised and abhorred by the nation, to the servant of rulers: "Kings will see you and rise up, princes will see and bow down, because of the LORD, who is faithful, the Holy One of Israel, who has chosen you."

Israel's future Ruler would be the one to whom kings and princes would someday bow down. Israel's "exaltation" is in reality the exaltation of her God and Savior (see also Isaiah 60:14). The Gentiles are subjected only in the sense of spiritual submission to the Lord.

The Gentiles Join in the Worship of the God of Israel

The Gentiles join Israel, not to share in a political amalgamation, but to share in the worship of the God of Israel–the one true and living God. It was because of the Messiah, "a leader and commander for the peoples," that nations would "run" to Israel (Isaiah 55:4-5). Isaiah 19:18-22 pictures the conversion of Egypt in highly figurative terms. Five cities in Egypt would speak the language of Canaan and swear allegiance to the Lord (19:18).

An altar and pillar would be erected to the Lord (19:19), and sacrifices and offerings would be given (19:21). Isaiah 19:23-25 carries the picture even further, and portrays Egypt, Assyria, and Israel worshiping together. A "highway" (here it very clearly represents *spiritual access*) would connect Egypt and Assyria so that they could worship together (19:23). Isaiah concludes:

In that day Israel will be the third, along with Egypt and Assyria, a blessing on the earth. The LORD Almighty will bless them, saying, "Blessed be Egypt my people, Assyria my handiwork, and Israel my inheritance." (19:24-25)

Israel and her enemies are seen united one day in the worship of the Lord. The blessing of Israel will be the blessing of the nations (see Genesis 12:3; Galatians 3:8). The picture here is not one of Gentile subjection, but one of spiritual unity under the Messiah.

The prophet Zechariah offers a very colorful description of the Gentiles' conversion in Zechariah 8:20-23. The key element is that these nations come to Jerusalem in order to seek the Lord. The description of a crowd of Gentiles grabbing a lone Jew is particularly effective:

> This is what the LORD Almighty says: "In those days ten men from all languages and nations will take firm hold of one Jew by the hem of his robe and say, 'Let us go with you, because we have heard that God is with you.'" (Zechariah 8:23)

Also in Zechariah 6:15, a very significant promise is made. Haggai promised to those returnees from Babylon who were trying to rebuild an "economy model" of the earlier temple, that "the latter glory of this house will be greater than the former" (Haggai 2:9). This would be due to Gentile participation (2:8). Zechariah describes this building of a future temple, one which would far exceed the glory of the one under construction (Zechariah 6:15). The New Testament clearly reveals that the Gentiles in the church age are presently building God's temple: Ephesians 2:19-22.

Two approaches are available to the interpreter when comparing Zechariah 6:15 and Ephesians 2:19-22. One is to recognize that while Paul's language is figurative, it fulfills the intent of Zechariah so that the latter should also be taken in a figurative sense. This is interpreting a difficult passage in light of a clear one. The second approach is to presuppose that Zechariah is speaking of a literal temple, and since Paul's temple is figurative, then the two have no connection whatsoever. The building of the temple by the Gentiles, then, is still future. This method, that of the dispensationalists, insists upon hyperliteral interpretations of obviously figurative language, and often ignores the clear New Testament evidence for a proper interpretation.

The Gentiles Bring Their Wealth to Israel

Included in the worship of the Gentiles is the bringing of their wealth to the God of Israel. It is because of this great influx of wealth that the latter glory of the "temple" will be greater than the former (Haggai 2:7-9). Those who share in Israel's glorious future will "eat the wealth of nations" and boast in their riches (Isaiah 61:6). This privilege is related to the fact that they would then be "priests of the Lord" (6:16; see Exodus 19:6; I Peter 2:9).

The rich imagery of Isaiah 60 totally defies a literal interpretation. Because of the light that has come to Israel, the rest of the world, shrouded in deep darkness, begins to come toward that shining light (60:1-3). Israel receives the "wealth of the nations" and the "abundance of the sea" (60:5). Included in this massive "economic boom" are camels from Midian and Ephah, gold and frankincense from Sheba, the flocks of Kedar, the rams of Nebaioth, and silver and gold from Tarshish (60:6-9). The flow of incoming riches would be continuous:

> Your gates will always stand open, they will never be shut, day
> or night, so that men may bring you the wealth of the nations–their
> kings led in triumphal procession. (Isaiah 60:11)

Those who do not willingly share in the worship of Israel's God will perish (60:12). The picture of Zion in verse 16 is that of a nursing child feeding on the choicest products of the nations: "You will also suck the milk of nations, and will suck the breasts of kings" (60:16; cf. 66:10-13). Should not literalists who are overly concerned with prophetic real estate, livestock, slave labor, dollars and shekels, etc., now include pints and ounces in their computations?

The Gentiles Greatly Enlarge Israel

The conversion of the Gentiles not only contributes to Israel's "exaltation," but also to her remarkable enlargement. The picture is of a land too cramped for her inhabitants (Isaiah 49:19; also Zechariah 10:10).

Divine Increase

Israel's children would one day say, "The place is too cramped for me; make room for me that I may live here" (49:20). The natural question raised in the minds of down-trodden Israel would concern the origin of this sudden increase:

> Then you will say in your heart, "Who bore me these? I was be-
> reaved and barren; I was exiled and rejected. Who brought these up?
> I was left all alone, but these–where have they come from?" (49:21)

The answer provided is the picture of the conversion of the Gentiles.

> This is what the Sovereign LORD says: "See, I will beckon to the Gentiles, I will lift up my banner to the peoples; they will bring your sons in their arms and carry your daughters on their shoulders. Kings will be your foster fathers, and their queens your nursing mothers. They will bow down before you with their faces to the ground; they will lick the dust at your feet. Then you will know that I am the LORD; those who hope in me will not be disappointed." (49: 22-23).

A similar promise is found in Isaiah 54 where it is stated, "For the sons of the desolate one will be more numerous than the sons of the married woman," says the Lord (54:1b). The picture here, however, is of a tent being enlarged to accommodate the great increase of people Israel would "spread out": "For you will spread abroad to the right and to the left. And your descendants will possess nations, and they will resettle the desolate cities" (54:3).

Messianic Conquest

Amos similarly describes Israel's possession of "Edom" and "all the nations who are called by My name" (Amos 9:12). There are some, no doubt, who would relegate this to the low level of a political and military conquest. The claim that these "captured" nations are called by God's own "name," however, suggest a spiritual union with Israel.

This incredible phenomenon, the incorporation of other nations into Israel itself, is the obvious explanation for Israel's great expansion, not geographically, but spiritually. Isaiah predicts the same thing in a slightly different way: "In the days to come Jacob will take root, Israel will blossom and sprout; and they will fill the whole world with fruit" (Isaiah 27:6).

Note Well: All students of Scripture have a basic agreement on the concept of "typology," although disagreements may exist on some of the particulars. In essence, a "type" (Greek TYPOS, "pattern, model") is an Old Testament person, event, institution, or thing that has a divinely intended New Testament correspondence. The New Testament fulfillment of such a typical correspondence is called the "antitype" (Greek ANTI-, "against" or, as here, "instead of"). Examples of the type-antitype relationships in the Bible include Moses-Christ; Adam-Christ; passover lamb-Christ; David-Christ; Elijah-John the Baptist; Jonah's experience in the great fish-Christ's burial and resurrection; Noah's flood-the Second Coming; Noah's flood-Christian baptism; Melchizedek-Christ; Joshua (two of them)-Christ; and many others.

What has not been recognized by some students of Scripture, however, is that prophecies regarding various "types" are at times described *in the language of the "types."* The key example for us here is the David-Christ typology. Since Christ is the messianic "David," it would be natural for the Old Testament to describe him as doing "David-like" things. Doesn't that make good sense? Isaiah 11 provides a great picture of images to observe and test such a theory. In Isaiah 11, the future reign and work of the Messiah is described.

> 1 A shoot will come up from the stump of Jesse; from his roots a Branch will bear fruit.
> 2 The Spirit of the LORD will rest on him– the Spirit of wisdom and of understanding, the Spirit of counsel and of power, the Spirit of knowledge and of the fear of the LORD–
> 3 and he will delight in the fear of the LORD. He will not judge by what he sees with his eyes, or decide by what he hears with his ears;
> 4 but with righteousness he will judge the needy, with justice he will give decisions for the poor of the earth. He will strike the earth with the rod of his mouth; with the breath of his lips he will slay the wicked.
> 5 Righteousness will be his belt and faithfulness the sash around his waist.
> 6 The wolf will live with the lamb, the leopard will lie down with the goat, the calf and the lion and the yearling together; and a little child will lead them.
> 7 The cow will feed with the bear, their young will lie down together, and the lion will eat straw like the ox.
> 8 The infant will play near the hole of the cobra, and the young child put his hand into the viper's nest.
> 9 They will neither harm nor destroy on all my holy mountain, for the earth will be full of the knowledge of the LORD as the waters cover the sea.
> 10 In that day the Root of Jesse will stand as a banner for the peoples; the nations will rally to him, and his place of rest will be glorious. (Isaiah 11:1-10)

Later verses in this chapter are fascinating:

> He will raise a banner for the nations and gather the exiles of Israel; he will assemble the scattered people of Judah from the four quarters of the earth. Ephraim's jealousy will vanish, and Judah's enemies will be cut off; Ephraim will not be jealous of Judah, nor Judah hostile toward Ephraim. They will swoop down on the slopes

of **Philistia** to the west; together they will plunder the people to the east. They will lay hands on **Edom** and **Moab**, and the **Ammonites** will be subject to them. (Isaiah 11:12-14)

Ephraim (the Northern Kingdom) and Judah (the Southern Kingdom) will be re-united, just as they existed as one nation in David's day. But what about the Philistines, Ammonites, Edomites and Moabites? *These were neighboring enemy nations that David conquered during his reign.* Where are these nations today? Gone. Beware the trap of just matching ancient nations up with their modern geographical correspondences. Modern Jordan is not Moab!

Here's the connection. Just as David conquered these nations (here representing the Gentile nations as a whole, as elsewhere), so the *New David will conquer* them. But *spiritually*, not militarily. Ponder this concept, for to fail to grasp it, I believe, is to be doomed to failure in the study of Messianic Kingdom prophecy!

Conclusion

The prophetic theme involving God's future hope for the nations was a rich one indeed. Highly figurative language was often employed to speak to the prophets' audience in terms they would understand. To claim, as do dispensationalists, that the Old Testament in no way predicts the conversion of Gentiles into the church (the New Covenant "Israel"), flies in the face of what the Bible clearly teaches. The Rapture System's claim to "literal interpretation" apparently pertains to the Old Testament, not the New. That is unfortunate, since the New Testament is quite clear on the subject, as any reasonable system of interpretation would recognize.

Rapture Woe #8

The use of typological language for messianic prophecy means that military-sounding "conquests" actually refer to the spiritual conquest of the nations–their conversion, that is. The "New David" will do "David-like" things. Future military conquests for Israel are not what the Bible is describing.

7

THE TIMES OF THE SIGNS

Constant reminders of the principle are everywhere: "Timing is everything." All of us can no doubt attest to the value of correct timing in such areas as athletic competition, social events, personal relationships or business ventures. But when it comes to the time of Christ's return, Scripture's admonitions are clear: No one knows the day or the hour (or, I would add, the week, month, or even the year–Remember 88 *Reasons Why the Rapture Will Be in 1988* back in 1988?). Jesus warns his disciples,

> No one knows about that day or hour, not even the angels in heaven, nor the Son, but only the Father. Be on guard! Be alert! You do not know when that time will come. It's like a man going away: He leaves his house and puts his servants in charge, each with his assigned task, and tells the one at the door to keep watch. Therefore keep watch because you do not know when the owner of the house will come back–whether in the evening, or at midnight, or when the rooster crows, or at dawn. If he comes suddenly, do not let him find you sleeping. What I say to you, I say to everyone: "Watch!" (Mark 13:32-37)

One of the most basic issues regarding various prophetic views comes down to the timing of key events predicted in Scripture. The answer given concerning the timing of an event may radically influence our understanding of the nature of that event as well. No biblical book's interpretation is affected more by the question of timing than the book of Revelation. This chapter will close with an important discussion about how that book should be understood, and how that impacts the entire end-times debate. The answers given to the question of timing by students of prophecy may vary widely, as this and the next few chapters will make evident.

Which Day and Which Hour?

I appreciate the basic tone of John MacArthur's chapter "Does Any-body Really Know What Time It Is?" in his book *The Second Coming*. He rejects the speculative and potentially harmful practices of the "date-setters." As well, he notes the value in God's hiding from us the timing of Christ's return. If the hour were known, he suggests, "We would lose that balance of both expectancy and patience God commands us to maintain" (p. 139).

But MacArthur has some formidable problems to overcome in view of his Rapturist approach to Scripture. Language that we would expect to apply to the "any-moment Rapture" instead at times points more to the so-called "Revelation" of Christ, Christ's return to earth in judgment. Since the Rapture System teaches that the so-called "Rapture" could occur *at any moment*, the Biblical teaching of the imminency of Christ's return is thus "protected." Sounds good so far. No specific signs are viewed as yet necessary to unfold prior to Jesus' coming for His church. Like a "thief in the night" He will unexpectedly descend and His followers will rise to meet Him in the air. The rest will be "left behind." According to this approach, everything is now in place for the Rapture events to unfold. No countdown is needed or possible.

However, upon closer examination, the Rapturists' distinction be-tween the descriptions of the "Rapture" and the subsequent (seven years later) "Revelation" of Christ quickly breaks down. The Olivet Discourse, the focal point of MacArthur's book *The Second Coming*, clearly demon-strates this failed distinction. You see, the problem with the above Mark 13 quote is that it allegedly refers to the Second Coming ("Revelation") that follows by 3½ years the "Abomination of Desolation," which itself will have followed the secret Rapture of the church by 3½ years. From the time of the Rapture to the Revelation of Christ will be a literal seven-year period, according to their system. Where's the "not knowing" here?

The problem should be obvious. Jesus' warnings should be under-stood as being directed to his disciples (including us!) in preparation for His return at the end of *this* age, not at the later end of the alleged "Tribu-lation Period." When Rapturists place the "Coming of the Son of Man"

3½ years after the Great Tribulation, which in turn was 3½ years after the secret (but noisy!) Rapture, all kinds of problems emerge.

This becomes more obvious when the longer parallel passage in Matthew 24 is examined (another account of Jesus' Olivet Discourse).

Immediately after the distress of those days "the sun will be darkened, and the moon will not give its light; the stars will fall from the sky, and the heavenly bodies will be shaken." At that time the sign of the Son of Man will appear in the sky, and all the nations of the earth will mourn. **They will see the Son of Man coming on the clouds of the sky, with power and great glory.** And he will send his angels with a loud trumpet call, and they will gather his elect from the four winds, from one end of the heavens to the other. (Matthew 24:29-31)

No one knows about that day or hour, not even the angels in heaven, nor the Son, but only the Father. As it was in the days of Noah, so it will be at the coming of the Son of Man. For in the days before the flood, people were eating and drinking, marrying and giving in marriage, up to the day Noah entered the ark; and they knew nothing about what would happen until **the flood came and took them all away.** That is how it will be at the coming of the Son of Man. **Two men will be in the field; one will be taken and the other left.** Two women will be grinding with a hand mill; one will be taken and the other left. Therefore keep watch, because **you do not know on what day your Lord will come.** But understand this: **If the owner of the house had known at what time of night the thief was coming, he would have kept watch** and would not have let his house be broken into. So you also must be ready, because **the Son of Man will come at an hour when you do not expect him.** (Matthew 24:36-44)

The Coming of the Son of Man that Jesus is talking about here would involve signs in the heavens, the mourning of the nations, the removal of the wicked—as believers and unbelievers are separated for all eternity, and the unexpectedness of a thief in the night. Clearly a separate pre-tribulational Rapture for the church is not involved in this passage.

From the their entire treatment of the Olivet Discourse, the Rapturists have made it clear that Jesus *was indeed* talking now about His Second Coming, what they view to be the "Revelation" at the end of the alleged Great Tribulation. That is what they have tried to maintain that this text is all about. I believe that they are dead wrong, but it is *their* position. However, that doesn't stop Tim LaHaye from flip-flopping time zones and attempting to "smuggle" this language back to the events *before* the Rapture of the church. Under the heading "The Rapture Is Imminent," LaHaye explains,

> One of the chief characteristics of the Rapture of the church is that it will be sudden, unexpected, and will catch people by surprise. Some students of Scripture will anticipate "the season" or general period, but as our Lord said, "No man knows the day or the hour." Which is why we should so live as to "be ready, for the Son of Man is coming at an hour when you do not expect Him" (Matthew 24: 44). **Only the pre-Tribulation rapture preserves that at-any-moment expectation of His coming.** (*Are We Living in the End Times?*, p. 116)

Look at that last line carefully! LaHaye's problem is that the coming that Jesus is talking about is *not* the Rapture. It's the "post-Tribulation" Second Coming. LaHaye and other adherents to the Rapture System claim that they, unlike amillennialists and other spiritualizers of Scripture, take the Bible "at face value" and accept the *clear* meaning of the text. After much study of their disjointed and contradictory interpretations, I can assure you that there is little clear about all the "cut-and-paste" methods that they have employed in order to "rightly divide the Word of Truth" according to their dispensational framework. Here LaHaye has applied Jesus' words supposedly spoken about his post-tribulational Revelation to the alleged *pre*-tribulational Rapture. Is that fair?

To Catch a Thief

One problem, among others, is that Rapturists can't *find* a "thief in the night" *Rapture* text anywhere! The language always relates to the "glorious appearing" that accompanies scenes of judgement or the ushering in of the Eternal State.

> For you know very well that **the day of the Lord will come like a thief in the night**. While people are saying, "Peace and safety," **destruction will come on them suddenly,** as labor pains on a pregnant woman, and they will not escape. But you, brothers, are not in darkness so that **this day should surprise you like a thief.** (1 Thessalonians 5:2-4)

> **But the day of the Lord will come like a thief.** The heavens will disappear with a roar; the elements will be destroyed by fire, and the earth and everything in it will be laid bare. (2 Peter 3:10)

> Then I saw three evil spirits that looked like frogs; they came out of the mouth of the dragon, out of the mouth of the beast and out of the mouth of the false prophet. They are spirits of demons performing miraculous signs, and they go out to the kings of the whole world, to gather them for the battle on the great day of God Almighty. **"Behold, I come like a thief! Blessed is he who stays awake and keeps his clothes with him, so that he may not go naked and be shamefully exposed."** Then they gathered the kings together to the place that in Hebrew is called Armageddon. (Revelation 16:13-16)

Odd, isn't it, that the coming of Jesus which follows a host of signs and warnings, the one seven years after the Rapture and 3½ years after the Great Tribulation, is the "thief-in-the-night" return? How unlikely that is. It sounds like the "thief-in-the-night" return spoken of in the New Testament is *seven years too late* to apply to the Rapture. But who's counting?

Oops, wait a minute, make that *1,000 years* too late, or, to be more precise, 1,007 years. 2 Peter 3 connects the Lord Jesus' coming "like a thief" with the conflagration of this present order and the creation of a "New Heaven and New Earth," what we might also refer to as the New Creation or the Eternal State. That creates a problem for the Rapture System. Several problems, actually. First, the "like a thief" language should be pointing to the Rapture. Second, the earth isn't supposed to be destroyed until after the thousand-year earthly Millennial Kingdom. Then there's the seven years between the Rapture and the Second Coming. (Actually, now Tim LaHaye thinks that there will be at least 10½ years or so between those events, because, really, all these numbers just really do not add up so well. Consistent hyperliteralism creates contradictions impossible for the Rapturists to resolve. See later the chapter "Agog Over Gog and Magog.")

The 2 Peter 3 solution? The Rapture System teaches that the "Day of the Lord" will begin with the Rapture, continue through the seven (10½?) years between the Rapture and the Second Coming, further continue through the entire thousand-year kingdom and then end with the ushering in of the Eternal State. What a "day"! Whatever happened to the insistence on literal interpretation?. It goes out the window when the System is in jeopardy. Now you know the drill.

Total Needed: ONE Second Coming

The correct understanding rather is that this "like a thief" language applies to the Second Coming, which is a *single*, not multi-stage event. This is the best way to understand the Bible's teaching on the subject, including what we read in 2 Thessalonians 1:6-10:

> God is just: He will pay back trouble to those who trouble you and give relief to you who are troubled, and to us as well. This will happen when the Lord Jesus is revealed from heaven in blazing fire with his powerful angels. He will punish those who do not know God and do not obey the gospel of our Lord Jesus. They will be punished with everlasting destruction and shut out from the presence of the Lord and from the majesty of his power on the day he comes to be glorified in his holy people and to be marveled at among all those who have believed. This includes you, because you believed our testimony to you.

Here we see two sides of the Second Coming. Not two comings separated by seven years and innumerable events on earth, but rather one unified return. For the faithful it will be "relief," "glorious," but for the wicked "punishment," "everlasting destruction." Especially note the "you" here in this text. Don't miss this. At the Second Coming, Christ will be "marveled at" by the church age Christians, not post-Rapture Tribulation saints. How can Paul's clear meanings be distorted so by today's interpreters?

Tribulation Countdown?

The next two chapters will show you where I stand on the so-called "Great Tribulation." I believe that the current popular understanding is far afield from what the Bible actually teaches. So when *does* the Great Tribulation take place?

LaHaye and Ice have said much about this alleged event:

> In His masterful Olivet Discourse, our Lord warned that this world has yet to see a time of "great tribulation, such as was not since the beginning of the world to this time, no, nor ever shall be" (Matthew 24:21 KJV). *And those who take the Bible literally find it significant that the Tribulation period is given more space in Scripture than any other comparable event.* [italics mine] There is more space allocated to the Tribulation than the 1000-year Millennial kingdom, heaven,

hell, or any subject except salvation and the promise of Christ's second coming. It is mentioned at least 49 times by Hebrew prophets and at least 15 times in the New Testament.

Old Testament Tribulation References

The Time of Jacob's Trouble . . . . . . Jeremiah 30:7
The Seventieth Week of Daniel . . . Daniel 9: 27
Jehovah's Strange Work . . . . Isaiah 28:21
Jehovah's Strange Act . . . . Isaiah 28:21
The Day of Israel's Calamity . . . . . . Deuteronomy 32:35; Obadiah 12-14
The Tribulation . . . . Deuteronomy 4:30
The Indignation . . . . Isaiah 26:20; Daniel 11:36
The Overflowing Scourge . . . . Isaiah 28:15, 18
The Day of Vengeance . . . . Isaiah 34:8; 35:4; 61:2
The Year of Recompense . . . . Isaiah 34:8
The Time of Trouble . . . . Daniel 12:1; Zephaniah 1:15
The Day of Wrath . . . . Zephaniah 1:15
The Day of Distress . . . . Zephaniah 1:15
The Day of Wasteness . . . . Zephaniah 1:15
The Day of Desolation . . . . Zephaniah 1:15
The Day of Darkness . . . . Zephaniah 1:15; Amos 5:18, 20;
Joel 2:2
The Day of Gloominess . . . . Zephaniah 1:15; Joel 2:2
The Day of Clouds . . . . Zephaniah 1:15; Joel 2:2
The Day of Thick Darkness . . . . . . Zephaniah 1:15, Joel 2:2
The Day of the Trumpet . . . . Zephaniah 1:16
The Day of Alarm . . . . Zephaniah 1:16

The details provided in all these Bible passages make it obvious that this is a future event, for no such period has yet occurred in human history. (*Charting the End Times*, p. 56)

Contrary to the claim, the above Scriptures taken literally do *not* support the dispensational Great Tribulation scenario. In fact, most of the Old Testament texts cited above are *totally irrelevant to the issue*. Check out the references and see for yourself. I do not understand how Bible expositors can get away with such escapades. It is baffling.

Let's take Zephaniah here as one example of dispensational abuse, since it is quoted so extensively in connection with the alleged future Great Tribulation, especially Zephaniah 1:15-16. No less than eleven explicit expressions are claimed to refer to the post-Rapture Great Tribulation. However, the earlier context in Zephaniah makes it clear that the "day of the Lord" being talked about here instead related to Judah's punishment at the hands of the Babylonians because of their idolatrous practices.

> I will stretch out my hand against Judah and against all who live in Jerusalem. I will cut off from this place every remnant of Baal, the names of the pagan and the idolatrous priests–those who bow down on the roofs to worship the starry host, those who bow down and swear by the LORD and who also swear by Molech, those who turn back from following the LORD and neither seek the LORD nor inquire of him. Be silent before the Sovereign LORD, for the day of the LORD is near. The LORD has prepared a sacrifice; he has consecrated those he has invited. On the day of the LORD's sacrifice I will punish the princes and the king's sons and all those clad in foreign clothes. On that day I will punish all who avoid stepping on the threshold, who fill the temple of their gods with violence and deceit. (Zephaniah 1:4-9)

Note the themes here: Baal worship, Molech (Milcom) worship, and other idolatrous practices. The princes and the king's sons are singled out. **It is obvious that these descriptions have absolutely nothing to do with a post-Rapture Great Tribulation.** Rapturists like LaHaye and others cannot cut-and-paste their way through prophetic texts like this and then claim that they are employing the literal, natural method of interpretation. Do you see the problem?

Revelation's Signs and Times

An extensive treatment of the book of Revelation cannot be attempted here. It is important to note, however, that as our understanding of the nature of ancient Jewish writings has grown, a greater awareness of the symbolic and practical nature of the book of Revelation is emerging. I believe that a virtual "revolution" is taking place in the modern understanding of this "apocalyptic" book. The next few years will see an increasing departure from the older perspectives of how Revelation should be understood and presented. This is not a move toward liberalism. It is a change in perception as to what forms and functions God's inspired Word originally had. We are getting ever closing to seeing this book as the first-century Christians must have viewed it.

An extended quote from Tony Campolo may help to illustrate this shift. He writes this in the Foreword to *Of Angels, Beasts, and Plagues,* a Revelation comentary by Kenneth H. Maahs (pp. xi-x).

When I was a teenager, the Revelation of Saint John the Divine provided me with endless fascination. I believed the book to be a coded message that, for those who understood it, could explain current events and even predict the future .... Whenever the minister of my church wanted to build up attendance at the Sunday evening services, all he had to do was announce that he would be doing a series on the book of Revelation. I was not the only one who wanted guided excursions into that exotic world of the seven churches of Asia, the whore of Babylon, and the awesome Antichrist. These Sunday evening services held the promise for everyone that our pastor would let us in on an array of "deep secrets," not the least of which would be a good reading about when to expect the second coming of Christ. After we heard our pastor's sermons, it seemed so obviously clear that we were living in the last days and that the Antichrist was already among us. The colorful charts that he used as he showed us "God's Plan for the Ages" left us deeply impressed with how fortunate we were to have a minister who was able to discern "the signs of the times."

After a while even a slow learner like me began to be suspicious as to whether or not these prophecy preachers really knew what they were talking about. Like Martin Luther, I became just plain cynical about all this kind of prophecy preaching from the book of Revelation; I decided that this last book of the Bible really was not worth my time and energy ....

Things are different now. In the not-too-distant past, some fellow Christians taught me a whole new way of reading the book of Revelation. They introduced me to the idea that this book was written in a very specialized genre common in the ancient world, called *apocalyptic literature.* According to this approach to understanding the book, there is still a need for decoding. But rather than understanding Revelation as a collection of prophecies of futuristic events, I came to see that this book could be a useful instrument for understanding what God wants to tell his people in every age, including our own. In coming to read the book of Revelation as apocalyptic literature, I found that I could learn from it crucial lessons about how to live, what to guard against in my everyday life, and how to understand what it means to live out Christianity as a countercultural lifestyle. Also, I have come to see that this book has a great deal to say to the church.

> What John said about the seven churches of Asia back there and
> then can be used as a typology to evaluate and understand churches
> at any time or place over the last two thousand years of church his-
> tory and especially our own.

"Things are different now," says Campolo. Indeed they are. Stay
tuned for future developments.

Tony Campolo is not alone in this understanding of how to approach
the book of Revelation. One of my colleagues at Ozark Christian College,
Mark Moore, has a written a devotional book on Revelation entitled *How
to Dodge a Dragon*. He speaks to the issue of the applicability of Revelation to all ages:

> But what if Revelation is not viewed as a calendar but as a
> template? What if we are able to lay its principles over any period
> of suffering? Then most Christians throughout the history of the
> church who have applied Revelation to themselves have been mostly
> right. That is not to say that John did not have a historic reality in
> mind when he wrote the book. It is to say, however, that like the
> prophecies of the Old testament, there are principles and metaphors
> imbedded in them that are contemporary and relevant for each gen-
> eration. That's why this book has perpetual relevance. Wherever
> there is tragedy or suffering, persecuted Christians or rampant evil,
> this book weaves its way into the life of the church, reminding God's
> people of their security in Christ, the seriousness of their spiritual
> warfare, and the wondrous sovereignty of our mighty God. (*How to
> Dodge a Dragon*, p. 8)

We view the book of Revelation as containing much symbolic language, a characteristic that other apocalyptic works during New Testament times shared (e.g., the book of Enoch, Fourth Esdras, the Baruch
Apocalypse). What makes Revelation stand out among other books of
the same apocalyptic genre, however, is its inspired nature. God has
used various specific literary structures to convey His Word, including
hymnic poetry, treaty formulations, proverbs, genealogies, and epistles.
Apocalyptic symbolism was another. Figures and symbols certainly were
evoked from the imperial Roman setting of the book and the threat Rome
("Babylon") posed to the church. Certain emperors indeed were "beasts,"
and fanciful legends grew around them, legends that became common
knowledge, that may be reflected in the book. The use of Old Testament
imagery is extensive and profound. Cycles unfold throughout the book,
negating any notion of a consecutive forward storyline.

That is all that can be said at the present. Let me make one important application, however. If the approach lightly traced here be accepted in principle, then no end-times doctrine or scenario of specific events should rest solely upon the "evidence" from the book of Revelation. What we "know" from the book of Revelation about how end-times events will unfold may not be as much as many think. Certainly some caution should be exercised.

Rapture Woe #9

The more careful Rapturists teach that the "left behind" texts are not talking about the Rapture at all, but rather the later Revelation, and that those left behind are actually the righteous, not the wicked!

8

JESUS AND THE
END TIMES (I)

The importance of Jesus' teaching on the end times for the Rapture debate cannot be overestimated. Any view that does not mesh with what Jesus taught must be jettisoned. Of all the teachings Christ did on the subject, none are more crucial than those that comprise what Bible students now refer to as the Olivet Discourse (Matthew 24; Mark 13; Luke 21). This address given by our Lord during the "Final Week" has become a battleground between various millennial persuasions. Sad, isn't it? But the implications of what Jesus said here are critical for our correct understanding of future (and *past*) events. This portion of Scripture must be examined carefully in light of so many unwarranted claims based on these verses.

Matthew, Mark and Luke are sometimes referred to as the "synoptic" Gospels, because they tend to look at the life of Christ similarly ("see along with"). The Gospel of John, on the other hand, contains significant additional information about Jesus' life and ministry. Gospel "harmonies" are published that show these three synoptic Gospels side by side, revealing all the similarities and differences in detail. The Olivet Discourse is somewhat unique, however, in that there is debate among students of prophecy as to whether these three Gospel writers are actually talking about the same events and circumstances.

I personally believe that it is in its convoluted treatment of Jesus' Olivet Discourse that the Rapture System most clearly shows its willingness to twist the clear sense of Scripture to serve its own ends. A quick glance at a few verses will illustrate the problem.

* **"Then let those who are in Judea flee to the mountains."**
(Mattthew 24:16; Mark 13:14; Luke 21:23)
* **"How dreadful it will be in those days for pregnant women and nursing mothers!"** (Matthew 24:19; Mark 13:17; Luke 21:23)

These verses are but several from a large number of verses in Matthew, Mark and Luke that say the same or virtually the same thing in all three Gospels. Unless there would be extraordinary reasons to believe otherwise, one would conclude that all three Gospels are speaking of the same events. *The Rapture System teaches something much different, however.* For dispensationalists, the focus of Matthew and Mark are quite different from Luke. Matthew and Mark (quoting Jesus) are speaking of the supposed events following the Rapture of the church and in connection with the "Great Tribulation" attack of the Antichrist upon the Jewish nation whom he has deceived and betrayed. This is when the "abomination of desolation" will occur in connection with the Jerusalem temple that allegedly will be rebuilt sometime right before or after the Rapture (*not* to be confused, naturally, with the "desolation" of Jerusalem mentioned in the *parallel verse* in Luke!). The disciples listening to Jesus are allegedly referred to "you" as representatives of these post-church-age believers.

Luke (also quoting Jesus), on the other hand, is speaking of events in connection with Jerusalem's first-century demise. The apostles as "you" represent the early Jewish Christians who will face troubled times in the years immediately following. But how can this be? Did Jesus give teaching regarding the years shortly to follow (Luke) and then, using often the identical language, talk about the "post-Rapture" age (Matthew and Mark)? Or did He just say it once (with normal expanding, gesturing) and the disciples through the inspiration of God could then figure out that the descriptions had a two-fold application? *Neither* explanation is very convincing, in my view.

The format below is designed to help you see for yourself. Are Jesus' teachings on the Mt. of Olives supportive of the Rapture System, or do they tell a different tale? Many of the so-called signs prior to Christ's return are pulled out of this passage. **If the understanding presented in this book is correct, these alleged signs disappear.** Which is it?

Matthew 24	Mark 13	Luke 21
1 Jesus left the temple and was walking away when his disciples came up to him to call his attention to its buildings.	1 As he was leaving the temple, one of his disciples said to him, "Look, Teacher! What massive stones! What magnificent buildings!"	5 Some of his disciples were remarking about how the temple was adorned with beautiful stones and with gifts dedicated to God. But Jesus said,
2 "Do you see all these things?" he asked. "I tell you the truth, not one stone here will be left on another; every one will be thrown down."	2 "Do you see all these great buildings?" replied Jesus. "Not one stone here will be left on another; every one will be thrown down."	6 "As for what you see here, the time will come when not one stone will be left on another; every one of them will be thrown down."

The Jerusalem temple rebuilt and expanded by Herod the Great was one of the wonders of the ancient world. The extensive temple mount was a massive construction that also functioned as an impenetrable fortress. And since it represented God's dwelling, the words of Jesus must have been almost inconceivable to his disciples. Jesus earlier had uttered made similar warnings, although the extent of the audience is not clear:

> As he approached Jerusalem and saw the city, he wept over it and said, "If you, even you, had only known on this day what would bring you peace–but now it is hidden from your eyes. The days will come upon you when your enemies will build an embankment against you and encircle you and hem you in on every side. They will dash you to the ground, you and the children within your walls. They will not leave one stone on another, because you did not recognize the time of God's coming to you." Then he entered the temple area and began driving out those who were selling. (Luke 19:41-45)

All commentators agree that in the references to not one stone being left upon the other Jesus was alluding to the destruction of Jerusalem in A.D. 70. From this point on, however, there is not much agreement on anything! I would suggest that this is not so much because Jesus' words were hopelessly obscure, but rather because readers are hindered by their particular systems of prophetic interpretation. The synoptic "look alike" Gospel accounts present challenges here, to be sure, but I believe that there are a couple of interpretative keys that may help us unlock the key elements and the focus of what Jesus was presenting.

Matthew 24	Mark 13	Luke 21
3 As Jesus was sitting on the Mount of Olives, the disciples came to him privately. "Tell us," they said, "when will this happen, and what will be the sign of your coming and of the end of the age?"	3 As Jesus was sitting on the Mount of Olives opposite the temple, Peter, James, John and Andrew asked him privately, 4 "Tell us, when will these things happen? And what will be the sign that they are all about to be fulfilled?"	7 "Teacher," they asked, "when will these things happen? And what will be the sign that they are about to take place?"

The rest of the discourse was given from the vantage point of a spot on the side of the Mt. of Olives where Jesus and his disciples could look down and admire the magnificent temple and temple mount. Mark tells us that the words were actually given to the inner circle of disciples: Peter, James, John and Andrew. The questions here are worded slightly differently in the three Gospel records, but the first question in each is the same: When will this happen? It is critical to recognize that Jesus' disciples are asking *when the temple would be destroyed*. How can interpreters miss this obvious point? And yet the Rapture System teaches that, while the account in Luke speaks at least in part to the A.D. 70 fall of Jerusalem (at the very least Luke 21:20-24), *Matthew and Mark have nothing to say about that subject after verse 2!*

Of course, in the minds of the disciples, they were asking *one* basic question, even with Matthew's wording, since they assumed that such an event would only be possible in connection with the end of the age itself. But Jesus answers in such a way to make it clear to them that instead there were *two very distinct events on the horizon*: one near and accompanied with warning signs; the other at some point subsequent to the first and occurring without warning. I believe that this stark contrast is a major clue in helping solve the problem of what exactly Jesus was predicting.

Matthew 24	Mark 13	Luke 21
4 Jesus answered: "Watch out that no one deceives you. 5 For many will come in my name, claiming, 'I am the Christ,' and will deceive many.	5 Jesus said to them: "Watch out that no one deceives you. 6 Many will come in my name, claiming, 'I am he,' and will deceive many.	8 He replied: "Watch out that you are not deceived. For many will come in my name, claiming, 'I am he,' and, 'The time is near.' Do not follow them.

According to Jesus, who is in danger of being deceived? Who is the "you" being spoken of in the Olivet Discourse? I believe that at this very point the Rapturists are guilty of an indefensible slight of hand trick. The context obviously demands that the disciples themselves, or later Christians whom they represent, are the "you." The Rapture System demands otherwise. According to the "system," Jesus is addressing the future plight of post-Rapture tribulation saints! This is embarrassing exegesis, compelled by a misreading of Daniel 9 and the unfortunate results of the dispensational "postponement theory." A key element that has influenced their unlikely interpretation is the mention of the "Abomination of Desolation" and a "Great Tribulation." Rather than allowing the New Testament to be our guide in trying to get to the heart of what such terms mean, dispensationalists impose upon the New Testament their predetermined ideas of what these terms *must* mean, based on their hyperliteral exegesis of often difficult, poetic Old Testament prophecies.

One of the fine Old Testament scholars of our day is Gleason L. Archer. Although a dispensationalist, Archer holds to the mid-tribulational Rapture of the church, and sees many problems with the popular "Pretrib" view. He clearly does not understand Jesus' target audience to be a future *post-Rapture* generation. His lengthy observation bears quoting here.

> If the apostles and disciples who constituted the Christian church at the descent of the Holy Spirit on the Day of Pentecost were not true members or representatives of the Christian church, then who ever could be? Apart from the two books composed by Luke, the entire New Testament was composed by Jewish believers. For the first five years of the existence of the Christian church, during which several thousands of believers were added to its ranks, there was scarcely a non-Jew to be found in the entire company. All of the other admonitions and warnings addressed to the Twelve were unquestionably intended for them personally and found fulfilment or application in their later careers. How could it be that the Olivet

Discourse, and that alone, was an exception to this principle? How can we possibly imagine that when Christ said to His disciples, "These are the signs you are to look for," He really meant, "You will never see these signs at all, but 1900 years from now some distant descendants of yours are to look for these signs"? Such an interpretation as this appears to violate completely the principle of literal or normal interpretation that underlies the grammatical-historical exegesis of Scripture. We must of course compare other passages which bear upon this same theme as an aid to understanding this chapter aright, but we can scarcely go to the extreme of saying that Christ really meant the opposite of what He said. Yet if He addressed His remarks to nonexistent people who would not even be born until nineteen centuries later, then His Olivet Discourse boils down to: "Here are the signs you are to look for; but when I say 'you' I don't mean *you* but a future generation almost 2000 years in the future. And when I say, 'Look for these signs,' you are not to look for them, because you will not survive long enough to see them.'" This kind of interpretation adds up to a serious violation of the perspicuity [intelligibleness] of Scripture. We are bound to believe that when Jesus gave a prediction or a command, it was to be believed in and obeyed just as He expressed it, rather than in some arcane fashion discoverable only to those who were initiated into some specialized mode of interpretation not derivable from the text itself. (Gleason Archer in *The Rapture: Pre-, Mid-, or Post-Tribulational?*, pp. 123-124)

The classic pre-trib Rapture System has smuggled into this three-fold account of Jesus' teaching on the Mt. of Olives an interpretation that simply won't work. But it *must* work, if their Rapture doctrine is to be faithfully maintained! Which will it be? The clear intent of Scripture, or the unlikely scenarios created by the Rapturists?

Matthew 24	Mark 13	Luke 21
6 You will hear of wars and rumors of wars, but see to it that you are not alarmed. Such things must happen, but the end is still to come.	7 When you hear of wars and rumors of wars, do not be alarmed. Such things must happen, but the end is still to come.	9 When you hear of wars and revolutions, do not be frightened. These things must happen first, but the end will not come right away." 10 Then he said to them:
7 Nation will rise against nation, and kingdom against kingdom. There will be famines and earthquakes in various places.	8 Nation will rise against nation, and kingdom against kingdom. There will be earthquakes in various places, and famines.	"Nation will rise against nation, and kingdom against kingdom. 11 There will be great earthquakes, famines and pestilences in various places,
8 All these are the beginning of birth pains.	These are the beginning of birth pains.	and fearful events and great signs from heaven.

Within his discussion regarding the imminence question–the issue as to whether the New Testament teaches that Christ could return at any time, without future events needing to unfold–Gleason Archer makes a strong case for the fact that Jesus' apostles *could* have viewed the possibility of Jesus returning in their lifetime. In doing so he argues for what I believe Jesus is actually describing–first century events and crises. Regarding the disciples' expectations of Jesus' return in their generation, Archer writes (bold letters added):

> Can such an explanation be reconciled with an awareness of the fulfillment of prior signs? Yes it can, provided the world situation in apostolic times presented a set of factors resembling those described in the Olivet Discourse. Were there **false messiahs** at hand? Yes, there were some already at hand among the Jewish patriots during the build-up of resistance to Roman tyranny that culminated in the First Revolt (A.D. 66-70). During the Second Revolt, which occurred during the reign of Hadrian, Rabbi Akiba acclaimed Simon Barcochba as the Lord's Messiah. Were there **wars and rumors of war**? Even in the reign of Claudius and Nero there were frequent invasions and revolts that troubled the Empire. Were there **famines**? Yes, there was one so severe in Judea that Paul had to appeal to his new converts in Macedonia and Achaia to gather a relief fund for the starving Christian Jews of Palestine. Were there **earthquakes**? L.E. Toombs in *Interpreter's Dictionary of the Bible* 3:4, states, "Classical and modern authors record at least seventeen major earthquakes in the Palestine area during the Christian era." The geologic instability of the Jordan fault and the Mediterranean basin were illustrated by

the earthquake that accompanied the crucifixion and resurrection of Jesus (Matt. 27:54; 28:2) and the one that occurred at Philippi when Paul's jailor became converted (Acts 16:26). As for **hatred, persecution, and martyrdom of the saints**, these were already shaping up during Paul's own career of service, even prior to his ultimate execution in Rome under Nero. There were **serious factions** in the church at Corinth and **bitter contention** between leaders in various other centers. Hymenaeus and Philetus were teaching **heresy** (1 Tim. 1:20), and incipient Gnosticism gave rise to the Epistle to the Colossians. **The gospel was spreading throughout the Roman Empire** and even into Parthian domains with gratifying rapidity. **All of these developments fell into a pattern resembling the signs set forth in the Olivet Discourse, and so it was quite reasonable for the apostles themselves to consider the return of the Lord as a distinct possibility even in their own lifetime.** (Gleason Archer in *The Rapture: Pre-, Mid-, or Post-Tribulational?*, pp. 129-130)

The only way to make good sense of Jesus' teaching here is to view the conditions as described as being present in the first century, leading up to the "the end"–the fall of Jerusalem in A.D. 70. I'm not sure Archer wanted to make such a strong case for a first century focus!

Matthew 24:14
And this gospel of the kingdom will be preached in the whole world as a testimony to all nations, and then the end will come.

Find out why this is one of the most abused texts in the New Testament...

Matthew 24	Matthew 10	Mark 13	Luke 21
9 "Then you will be handed over to be persecuted and put to death, and you will be hated by all nations because of me.	17 "Be on your guard against men; they will hand you over to the local councils and flog you in their synagogues.	9 "You must be on your guard. You will be handed over to the local councils and flogged in the synagogues. On account of me you will stand before governors and kings as witnesses to them.	12 "But before all this, they will lay hands on you and persecute you. They will deliver you to synagogues and prisons, and you will be brought before kings and governors, and all on account of my name.
10 At that time many will turn away from the faith and will betray and hate each other,	18 On my account you will be brought before governors and kings as witnesses to them and to the Gentiles.	10 And the gospel must first be preached to all nations.	13 This will result in your being witnesses to them.
11 and many false prophets will appear and deceive many people.	19 But when they arrest you, do not worry about what to say or how to say it. At that time you will be given what to say,	11 Whenever you are arrested and brought to trial, do not worry beforehand about what to say. Just say whatever is given you at the time,	14 But make up your mind not to worry beforehand how you will defend yourselves.
12 Because of the increase of wickedness, the love of most will grow cold,	20 for it will not be you speaking, but the Spirit of your Father speaking through you.	for it is not you speaking, but the Holy Spirit.	15 For I will give you words and wisdom that none of your adversaries will be able to resist or contradict.
13 but he who stands firm to the end will be saved.	21 "Brother will betray brother to death, and a father his child; children will rebel against their parents and have them put to death.	12 "Brother will betray brother to death, and a father his child. Children will rebel against their parents and have them put to death.	16 You will be betrayed even by parents, brothers, relatives and friends, and they will put some of you to death.
14 And this gospel of the kingdom will be preached in the whole world as a testimony to all nations, and then the end will come.	22 All men will hate you because of me,	13 All men will hate you because of me,	17 All men will hate you because of me.
			18 But not a hair of your head will perish.
	but he who stands firm to the end will be saved.	but he who stands firm to the end will be saved.	19 By standing firm you will gain life.

Notice that in this section we show four accounts, not three. The teaching of the Olivet Discourse was not entirely new, apparently. Matthew 10 actually more closely parallels the Mark 13 and Luke 21 accounts here than does Matthew 24. Please note: **Matthew 10 was clearly addressed to the twelve apostles in connection with their own evangelistic efforts**. That should be decisive for our understanding of the "you" in Mark and Luke here (and in Matthew 24).

Matthew 24:14 is probably misapplied by most: "And this gospel of the kingdom will be preached in the whole world as a testimony to all nations, and then the end will come." THE END likely refers to Jerusalem's demise, the subject of the disciples' question. Jesus was indicating that by the time Jerusalem falls, Christianity will not be a localized Jewish sect, but a "worldwide" movement, unhindered by whatever catastrophe may befall the Jewish capital. The word OIKOUMENE, meaning "inhabited earth," is used in similar ways elsewhere, not necessarily indicating the entire globe. The census mentioned in Luke 2:1 was for the entire OIKOUMENE, "the entire *Roman* world." (The NIV added "*Roman*" here to help us properly limit the scope involved.) Jews at Pentecost came "from every nation under heaven" (Acts 2:5). If just some from each nation went back home with the gospel .... Also see Romans 1:8; 16:26; Colossians 1:6; 1:23. Phrases in connection with the first-century evangelizing efforts are found in these places, phrases like "all over the world" (Romans 1:8; Colossians 1:6) and "proclaimed to every creature under heaven" (Colossians 1:23). *If these words are not to be taken absolutely literally, then why must Jesus' words?*

Matthew 24	Mark 13	Luke 21
15 "So when you see standing in the holy place 'the abomination that causes **desolation**,' spoken of through the prophet Daniel– let the reader understand–	14 "When you see 'the abomination that causes **desolation**' standing where it does not belong– let the reader understand–	20 "When you see Jerusalem being surrounded by armies, you will know that its **desolation** is near.

Dispensationalists view their distinctive interpretation of Daniel 9, complete with the postponement of the 70th week, as a given. It is not. What we "know" Daniel says is used by them to bolster various premillennial interpretations of New Testament texts. Too much poorly done eschatology is blamed on Daniel. At Daniel 9:26 we read: "The people of the ruler who will come will destroy the city and the sanctuary. The end will come like a flood: War will continue until the end, and desolations have been decreed."

According to the Rapture System, the "people of the ruler who will come" are the Roman soldiers. The time? A.D. 70. However, "the ruler" himself is the Antichrist. The time? 3 1/2 years after the church is Raptured. A gap of nearly two thousand years so far. Is this a natural "face-value" approach to understanding Scripture? Rather it is an interpretation made desirable by a commitment to a Postponement Theory regarding the Kingdom.

The Hebrew of this section of Daniel is not easy and warrants a bit of caution. Ancient translations like the Greek Septuagint Bible and the eastern Christian Syriac Bible did *not* understand this verse as the dispensationalists today do. Nor did Josephus, as I intend to document at length in a future book, *The Man of Lawlessness and the Time of the End*. For now, his statements in *War of the Jews* may be consulted (4.6.3; 6.2.1).

Matthew 24	Mark 13	Luke 21
16 then let those who are in Judea flee to the mountains.	then let those who are in Judea flee to the mountains.	21 Then let those who are in Judea flee to the mountains, let those in the city get out, and let those in the country not enter the city.
17 Let no one on the roof of his house go down to take anything out of the house. 18 Let no one in the field go back to get his cloak.	15 Let no one on the roof of his house go down or enter the house to take anything out. 16 Let no one in the field go back to get his cloak.	
		22 For this is the time of punishment in fulfillment of all that has been written.
19 How dreadful it will be in those days for pregnant women and nursing mothers! 20 Pray that your flight will not take place in winter or on the Sabbath. 21 For then there will be **great distress**, unequaled from the beginning of the world until now–and never to be equaled again.	17 How dreadful it will be in those days for pregnant women and nursing mothers! 18 Pray that this will not take place in winter, 19 because those will be days of **distress** unequaled from the beginning, when God created the world, until now–and never to be equaled again.	23 How dreadful it will be in those days for pregnant women and nursing mothers! There will be **great distress** in the land and wrath against this people.
22 If those days had not been cut short, no one would survive, but for the sake of the elect those days will be shortened.	20 If the Lord had not cut short those days, no one would survive. But for the sake of the elect, whom he has chosen, he has shortened them.	24 They will fall by the sword and will be taken as prisoners to all the nations. Jerusalem will be trampled on by the Gentiles until the times of the Gentiles are fulfilled.

Again, you would think that the wording of Luke here would make it clear to all what Matthew and Mark are saying, but no such luck. Matthew 24:21 and Mark 13:19 are two of the most abused verses in all of Scripture. Dispensationalists hide behind the "never before-never again" language of our Lord to enable them to argue that the future so-called Great Tribulation, and not A.D. 70, is in Jesus' mind here. This is Bible exegesis at its worst. I am personally saddened by the inability of so many Bible "scholars" to see what is obvious in this text; but unfortunately an effort must now be made to make the point clear, so that others will not be trapped by the faulty and misleading arguments of the Rapture System.

Great Tribulation

The expression "great tribulation" (THLIPSIS MEGALE), called "great distress" here in the *New International Version*, has taken on a sense among modern prophecy buffs that it was never intended to have. It is presented by the Rapturist camp as a special term for the Antichrist's persecutions and God's outpouring of wrath that allegedly occurs after the Rapture. A word study of this expression and the term THLIPSIS alone, as Mark 13:19 has it, will reveal a wide range of applications. Some instances involve persecution of Christians, but not all. In Acts 7:11, THLIPSIS MEGALE refers to the severe famine in the time of Joseph in Egypt. Although the definite article in Greek can be a complicated issue, the lack of it at Matthew 24:21 suggests that it is not "THE Great Tribulation," whatever sense some give that, but just "great tribulation." The insistence that Jesus must be describing here a special end–times "Great Tribulation" has hindered students of the Word from seeing the obvious meaning of this section of the Olivet Discourse.

✓ Never to be Equaled

Unequaled? Unprecedented? Unparalleled? "Nothing like it before or after." Hmmm .... We read that same kind of language elsewhere in the Bible. The prophet Ezekiel said *the very same thing* about the Babylonian destruction of Jerusalem in 586 B.C.

> Therefore this is what the Sovereign LORD says: I myself am against you, Jerusalem, and I will inflict punishment on you in the sight of the nations. Because of all your detestable idols, **I will do to you what I have never done before and will never do again. Therefore in your midst fathers will eat their children, and children will eat their fathers. I will inflict punishment on you and will scatter all your survivors to the winds.** Therefore as surely as I live, declares the Sovereign LORD, because you have defiled my sanctuary with all your vile images and detestable practices, I myself will withdraw my favor; I will not look on you with pity or spare you. A third of your people will die of the plague or perish by famine inside you; a third will fall by the sword outside your walls; and a third I will scatter to the winds and pursue with drawn sword. Then my anger will cease and my wrath against them will subside, and I will be avenged. And when I have spent my wrath upon them, they will know that I the LORD have spoken in my zeal. (Ezekiel 5:8-13)

In the strictly literal sense that the Rapturists insist upon, how can 586 B.C. and A.D. 70 *both* be "never before-never again" calamities? Josephus even describes the cannibalism that likewise accompanied the later A.D. 70 siege.

Never before? What about the Noahic flood? How would that be surpassed by 586 B.C., or A.D. 70, or even the alleged Great Tribulation? Dispensationalists themselves actually offer us the solution to the whole problem they themselves have chosen to create. In a personal letter to fellow dispensationalist Thomas Ice, Arnold Fruchtenbaum responded to the point "The flood was obviously a greater Tribulation." His "able response" (according to Ice):

> This is true as far as Tribulation in general. However, here we are dealing specifically with the Jewish people and Jerusalem. The focus of the flood was not on the Jewish people, since Jewish history had not begun as yet. Nor was the focus on Jerusalem since that city had not existed yet. The Noahic flood destroyed the world in general and was the worst flood that ever was or will be. But Ezekiel's prophecy focuses specifically on the Jewish people and Jerusalem, which was not or will not be destroyed by flood (*The End Times Controversy*, p. 185).

Did you catch it? Fruchtenbaum's qualification: "*However, here we are dealing specifically with the Jewish people and Jerusalem.*" Exactly my point regarding Jesus' words at Matthew 24:21 and Mark 13:19, although I might substitute the words "Jewish nation" for Jewish people. This language cannot be used to justify the need for an end-times Tribulation that surpasses any of the horrors of modern times. The language deals with the unimaginable atrocities associated with the destruction of Jerusalem and the end of the Jewish nation in A.D. 70.

Never again? The worst health-related disaster within the last century was the Spanish flu. It infected some two billion people over the winter of 1918-1919 and left 30 million dead. What does this have to do with Jesus' words here? Nothing, of course. Or take World War II. The scope of the death and atrocities accompanying that conflict is mind numbing: **50 million dead**, including 20 million soldiers, 23 million civilians, and 7 million murdered. The number murdered included 1.5 million children. Of those 7 million murdered, 6 million were Jewish. What does all this have to do with Jesus' words here? Absolutely nothing.

To argue from the Holocaust that Jesus' words could not have been fulfilled in A.D. 70 is a tragic misinterpretation, in my view. I gladly part ways with the Rapturists who cannot get past the blind, inconsistent hyperliteralism that their system fosters.

Let's see what happens when we try to apply the dispensationalists' standards to the descriptions of good kings Hezekiah and Josiah in 2 Kings 18 and 23. Regarding Hezekiah we read,

> He did what was right in the eyes of the LORD, just as his father David had done. He removed the high places, smashed the sacred stones and cut down the Asherah poles. He broke into pieces the bronze snake Moses had made, for up to that time the Israelites had been burning incense to it. (It was called Nehushtan.) **Hezekiah trusted in the LORD, the God of Israel. There was no one like him among all the kings of Judah, either before him or after him. He held fast to the LORD and did not cease to follow him; he kept the commands the LORD had given Moses.** (2 Kings 18: 3-6)

Later of Josiah it was said,

> Furthermore, Josiah got rid of the mediums and spiritists, the household gods, the idols and all the other detestable things seen in Judah and Jerusalem. This he did to fulfill the requirements of the law written in the book that Hilkiah the priest had discovered in the temple of the LORD. **Neither before nor after Josiah was there a king like him who turned to the LORD as he did—with all his heart and with all his soul and with all his strength, in accordance with all the Law of Moses.** (2 Kings 23:24-25)

"No king like him—before or after." This is said of *both* Hezekiah and Josiah. I can live with such a seeming contradiction when a little poetic license and hyperbole are factored in. Can you?

As far as Jesus' words on the unequaled atrocities in connection with the A.D. 70 fall of Jerusalem, let's conclude with an eyewitness account of the terrible event. The Jewish historian Josephus was there when the siege pressed hard upon Jerusalem and its miserable populace. He speaks of the disaster in terms reminiscent of Jesus' own.

[handwritten margin note: Josephus' description of 70 AD]

> I shall therefore speak my mind here at once briefly: that **neither did any other city ever suffer such miseries**, nor did any age ever breed a generation more fruitful in wickedness than this was, **from the beginning of the world.** (*War of the Jews* 5.10.5)

Matthew 24	Mark 13	Luke 21
32 "Now learn this lesson from the fig tree: As soon as its twigs get tender and its leaves come out, you know that summer is near. 33 Even so, when you see all these things, you know that it is near, right at the door.	28 "Now learn this lesson from the fig tree: As soon as its twigs get tender and its leaves come out, you know that summer is near. 29 Even so, when you see these things happening, you know that it is near, right at the door.	29 He told them this parable: "Look at the fig tree and all the trees. 30 When they sprout leaves, you can see for yourselves and know that summer is near. 31 Even so, when you see these things happening, you know that the kingdom of God is near.
34 I tell you the truth, this generation will certainly not pass away until all these things have happened. 35 Heaven and earth will pass away, but my words will never pass away.	30 I tell you the truth, this generation will certainly not pass away until all these things have happened. 31 Heaven and earth will pass away, but my words will never pass away.	32 "I tell you the truth, this generation will certainly not pass away until all these things have happened. 33 Heaven and earth will pass away, but my words will never pass away.

I have included the Parable of the Fig Tree in this first chapter devoted to the Olivet Discourse. This is because these words take us back to what Jesus has devoted most of His teachings up to this point—the first-century fall of Jerusalem at the hands of the Romans. In each Gospel, the teaching here is set off by the same basic introduction: "Learn this lesson (PARABOLE) from the fig tree." This sets apart what follows as a distinct literary unit.

Much discussion is devoted by writers to the words "this generation." Rapturists must make this refer to the post-Rapture Tribulation saints (whom Jesus' disciples seem to represent by the word "you"). Much more likely is the view that Jesus is giving an extremely important time prophecy as a sign for His followers. His disciples' own generation would not pass away before His prophecies about Jerusalem were fulfilled. Forty years later, the Romans destroyed the city and the temple.

The reading of the *New International Version*, "it is near, right at the door," is to be preferred to "He is near ...." What is near is the time of Jerusalem's divine visitation in judgement at the hands of the Roman armies.

"When you see all these things" is conditioned by the context involving those events that will be accompanied by signs and warnings for them to escape. It does not have to refer to the unexpected, sudden Second Coming of Christ briefly described in the several verses previous. If that is understood, the discourse starts to make much better sense. Often in the Old Testament prophets there is a skipping back and forth between near and far events. (That is different from the common Rapturist claim that a single given prophecy can have multiple fulfillments. That questionable claim is the source of much abuse. If I don't "like" the way a prophecy has been fulfilled in the past–not literally enough, e.g.,–I can always posit a second future or "greater" fulfillment.)

This parable section, then, closes out Jesus' teaching on the fall of Jerusalem and includes the important warning to watch out for the warning signs. This distinguishes the A.D. 70 oracle from the Second Coming promises. As I intend to discuss in detail in the future, the expression "heaven and earth" may have been a Jewish expression to signify the temple itself! "Heaven and earth will pass away...."

9

JESUS AND THE END TIMES (II)

Immediately after the distress of those days "the sun will be darkened, and the moon will not give its light; the stars will fall from the sky, and the heavenly bodies will be shaken." At that time the sign of the Son of Man will appear in the sky, and all the nations of the earth will mourn. They will see the Son of Man coming on the clouds of the sky, with power and great glory. And he will send his angels with a loud trumpet call, and they will gather his elect from the four winds, from one end of the heavens to the other.
(Matthew 24:29-31)

If Jesus intended to address his disciples' questions with two distinct answers, one involving the A.D. 70 fall of Jerusalem and the other His Second Coming, a problem emerges. Where are the transitions in Matthew, Mark and Luke between these two events? Radically different answers have been given to that inquiry.

Of great importance to the question is the sense and significance of the word "immediately" (EUTHEOS) at Matthew 24:29. At first glance the term appears to be a roadblock for any idea of a transition from the first century to the last days. The coming of the Son of Man will occur "immediately after the distress of those days." How can that be true? First let's examine the two extremes on this subject—the views of the Rapturists and preterists.

In What Sense "Immediately"?

The Rapture System denies any reference to the first-century fall of Jerusalem after verse 2 in Matthew 24! In the previous chapter I have endeavored to explain the fallacies of that approach. The acceptance or rejection of the dispensational approach to Matthew 24 (and Mark 13) is a crossroads on one's personal journey in the study of Bible prophecy.

Dispensationalists understandably argue that Jesus' use of "immediately" supports their interpretation. To their thinking, the only way that the Second Coming could immediately follow the previous "abomination that desolates" and "great tribulation" would be if those events occurred right before the Second Coming. In the Rapture System, the disciples referred to as "you" in Matthew 24 represents the "Tribulation saints" on earth following the Rapture of the church. There must be a better explanation for the sense of "immediately" here!

The preterists come to the rescue here, but their "solution" creates even bigger problems. Full-blown preterism teaches that the time of Jerusalem's destruction was also the time of Christ's Second Coming. The preterist system cannot be discussed at length here. (I intend to spend more time on it in my upcoming *The Man of Lawlessness and the Time of the End*.) The denial of a future return of Christ has serious implications for our understanding of the Christian faith, of course. For one thing, how can the horrible events of the fall of Jerusalem be considered as the church's "Blessed Hope" (Titus 2:13)? Also, I definitely don't believe that the "New Heaven and New Earth" (2 Peter 3; Revelation 21-22) have already come into existence, do you? To an extent, the acceptance of preterism by some is an over-reaction to the Rapture System's many problems, but preterism itself also falls short of adequately dealing with the Bible's end-times teachings.

It is critical for the preterist position that all of the New Testament be written before A.D. 70, including the book of Revelation. Therefore the battle continues to rage over whether Revelation was written around the time of Nero (before A.D. 70) or Domitian (A.D. 95 or so). The evidence points to the later date and to the identification of "Babylon the harlot" as Rome, not Jerusalem—as preterists have tried to argue.

Naturally the expression "immediately" poses no problem for preterists, since for them the fall of Jerusalem description in the first part of the chapter is to be connected with language dealing with the coming of the Son of Man in the later portion. It is not clear to me, though, why this "coming" of Jesus is described as "immediately after" the great distress," if the destruction of Jerusalem at the hands of the Romans represents

Christ's coming in judgement in "flaming fire," etc. Why isn't it described as *during* the distress of those days?

Searching for a Better Idea

What about other options? Several suggestions have been given. Four approaches will be noted here.

(1) A common approach among both amillennialists and postmillennialists follows the preterist view in part. They argue that the "sky-is-falling"/"Jesus coming in the clouds" language is "apocalyptic" language and as such is used to describe the cataclysmic events surrounding the fall of Jerusalem. I would agree that this was indeed an "earth-shattering" event, especially when viewed from the perspective of the Jewish system and society. In their thinking, then, the transition to the Second Coming doesn't occur until Matthew 24:36, etc. I understand and appreciate the argument. But what do we do with the descriptions later in Matthew's account? If the fall of Jerusalem is described as Jesus coming on the clouds with His angels, with power and great glory (Matthew 24:330-31), then how does that differ from Matthew 25:31-32 in connection with the Sheep and Goats Judgement?

> When the Son of Man comes in his glory, and all the angels with him, he will sit on his throne in heavenly glory. All the nations will be gathered before him, and he will separate the people one from another as a shepherd separates the sheep from the goats.

What kind of "coming" will that be? The preterists press home the point that if the earlier description relates to A.D. 70, then so should the later one. I am not prepared to accept that the Sheep and Goats Judgement took place in the first century, and there is no need to do so. It is best not to view "the Son of Man coming on the clouds" as connected with the fall of Jerusalem.

(2) Some have proposed that we understand the adverb EUTHEOS in the sense of "suddenly" rather than "immediately." Emphasis on the suddenness of Jesus' return is found in the previous verses in Matthew 24 where the coming of the Son of Man is likened to the lightning flashing across the sky. That said, the usage of this Greek word in the New

Testament generally fits better the sense of immediacy, not suddenness, although the latter cannot be ruled out.

(3) Another option deserves consideration. It has been argued that "immediately" denotes something that can happen right away because there are no signs or events that must transpire before it takes place. In theological terms, the Lord's return is then *imminent*. Unlike the fall of Jerusalem, which had a number of warning signs preceding it, the Second Coming will be without warning, without precursor events. (Compare Luke 21:9, where Jesus said that, as signs of political turmoil began to emerge in the years ahead, the end–Jerusalem's fall–would *not* come EUTHEOS, "immediately.") In that sense then, Jesus' return can be viewed as occurring "immediately" after the great sign event of A.D. 70. Following the destruction of Jerusalem, all that was prophesied had been accomplished. The next great prophetic event on the horizon–Christ's return in glory.

(4) The following arrangement of verses is suggestive of yet another possible solution, as will now be explained. This solution sees merit especially in option "(3)" above, but also helps to soften some of the abruptness in the transition.

Matthew 24	Mark 13	Luke 21
23 At that time [THEN] if anyone says to you, 'Look, here is the Christ!' or, 'There he is!' do not believe it.	21 At that time [THEN] if anyone says to you, 'Look, here is the Christ!' or, 'Look, there he is!' do not believe it.	24 Jerusalem will be trampled on by the Gentiles until the times of the Gentiles are fulfilled.
24 For false Christs and false prophets will appear and perform great signs and miracles to deceive even the electBif that were possible. 25 See, I have told you ahead of time. 26 So if anyone tells you, 'There he is, out in the desert,' do not go out; or, 'Here he is, in the inner rooms,' do not believe it. 27 For as lightning that comes from the east is visible even in the west, so will be the coming of the Son of Man. 28 Wherever there is a carcass, there the vultures will gather.	22 For false Christs and false prophets will appear and perform signs and miracles to deceive the electBif that were possible. 23 So be on your guard; I have told you everything ahead of time.	

A Key Transition: the Aftermath of A.D. 70

Most commentators who try to distinguish between the A.D. 70 description and the Second Coming description place the break or transition at Matthew 24:29, the "immediately after" statement. (The similar transitions would be at Mark 13:24 and Luke 21:25, although the term EUTHEOS is not used.) I believe that this may be the wrong place to view the main transition. Instead I would suggest Matthew 24:23 (Mark 13:21). The Greek word TOTE may be translated "at that time," as here in the *New International Version*. However, it may also be translated "then," in the sense of what is about to happen next. Careful Greek studies in the Gospel of Matthew's usage of TOTE have demonstrated that this latter sense is Matthew's most frequent usage of this term.

If this is the case here, then the language of Matthew 24:23-28 is not a restatement of previous warnings, as many assume. Jesus is not repeating Himself. He is pointing to the aftermath of A.D. 70 and the continued trials the disciples would face. It is easy to lose sight of the complexity of the situation in which Jesus' followers would find themselves as the church age began. The events surrounding the revolt against Rome, A.D. 66-70, were the focus of Jesus' teachings about when His statement concerning the temple's destruction would be fulfilled. However, they were not the primary concern that Jesus addressed regarding his disciples.

Troublesome Times for Followers

Because of Jesus' warnings, the Judean Christians would know when it was time to abandon Jerusalem. But more importantly they were being prepared for the persecutions that would come from both Jew and Gentile. The years leading up to A.D. 70 would be tumultuous times for all, but for Christ's disciples they would be times of testing and testimony—testimony that would result in betrayals, arrests, trials, floggings, and even death. "All men will hate you because of me." (Matthew 24:22; Mark 13:13; Luke 21:17) Making their situation even more precarious would be the radical zealot uprising against Rome and the violent political unrest it would bring. These lawless ones, whom Josephus called simply "robbers," would make the Judean countryside a treacherous region, and Jerusalem, after thousands of them relocated within the city walls, a death trap.

In light of the great challenges facing His disciples in the decades immediately ahead, the dispensational notion that in Matthew (and Mark, and possibly Luke) Jesus is primarily addressing the future plight of the post-Rapture "Tribulation saints" becomes even more absurd. ("Absurd" is a strong word, to be sure, but I believe it fits the situation stated here.)

Although the fall of Jerusalem fulfills "the end" Jesus describes (Matthew 24:6, 14), it is not the end of the story for His followers. Some interpreters, such as the renown theologian B. B. Warfield, have argued that the fall of Jerusalem and the Jewish state signaled a time of greater vulnerability for the infant church, since it could not as easily hide under the umbrella of protection that Judaism provided within the Roman Empire. Now viewed as distinct from Jews, Christians were no longer exempt from required acts of pagan worship within the Roman Empire. Persecution of non-compliant Christians would follow.

Deceivers would continue to plague the church in the years to follow. False prophets and messianic pretenders would seek to lead God's elect astray. John could tell his "children" near the end of the first century, **"Many false prophets have gone out into the world"** (1 John 4: 1). Some leaders would be wolves in sheep's clothing (Matthew 7:5; Acts 20:29-30). Destructive heresies would be brought in (2 Peter 2:1ff). The spirit of "antichrist" was a reality by the end of the first century (1 John 2:18, 22: 4:3). False teachers would claim that Jesus had not come in the flesh (2 John 7). Hymenaeus and Philetus, Paul warned Timothy, were saying that the resurrection had already taken place (2 Timothy 2:17-18).

These would be difficult times, so Jesus wished to arm them beforehand with the necessary knowledge. (Again, how can Jesus' words, "See, I have told you ahead of time," in any reasonable way apply to post-Rapture Tribulation saints, while the early Christians are passed over?) No one would be able to claim to others that he had seen the Messiah, because when the Son of Man returns, all will see Him in an instant, as the lightning flashes from east to west.

"Wherever there is a carcass, there the vultures will gather." Even amidst the rugged Judean terrain, the remains of a dead animal could easily be located, since the circling vultures clearly marked the spot. When it comes to His return, Jesus is saying, "You can't miss it!"

Some confusion has arisen because of the choice of several translations to use the word "eagle" instead of "vulture." The eagle was a symbol used by the Roman armies, and so the conclusion has been that Jesus is describing here the carcass, Jerusalem, being surrounded by the Roman "eagles." Instead, the word "vulture" best fits the context and the expression serves to describe the Second Coming, not Jerusalem's destruction, as its further usage at Luke 17:24, 37, testifies.

The Rest of the Story

Summarizing, this section at Matthew 24:23-27 is not just a recap of what has already been said, but rather points ahead to additional tribulation for the people of God. The disciples wanted to know when the temple would be destroyed. Jesus, in His answer, wanted them to know the "rest of the story." Their future as followers of Jesus the Messiah would have very little to do with that great edifice that adorned the city of Jerusalem. The "tribulation" of Jerusalem would be quite different from the tribulation Jesus' disciples would face. The timing of "the restoration of the kingdom to Israel?" they later wondered ... (Acts 1:6). Jesus, just days before Pentecost and the establishment of the church, again told them what they needed to know:

> It is not for you to know the times or dates the Father has set by his own authority. But you will receive power when the Holy Spirit comes on you; and you will be my witnesses in Jerusalem, and in all Judea and Samaria, and to the ends of the earth. (Acts 1:7-8)

"You will be my witnesses." The disciples' old agendas and timetables were out the window. God was creating a new thing on earth. A new chapter in His redemptive purposes was about to unfold. He would make of Jew and Gentile a new creation, bringing peace and community and holiness of life (Ephesians 2:15ff). *"To the ends of the earth."* According to the record of the New Testament, and as obedient testimony to our Lord's commands, these words were being fulfilled even before the walls of Jerusalem and the structures of Judaism came tumbling down.

Matthew 24	Mark 13	Luke 21
29 "Immediately after the distress of those days" the sun will be darkened, and the moon will not give its light;	24 "But in those days, following that distress, "'the sun will be darkened, and the moon will not give its light;	25 "There will be signs in the sun, moon and stars. On the earth, nations will be in anguish and perplexity at the roaring and tossing of the sea.
the stars will fall from the sky, and the heavenly bodies will be shaken.'	25 the stars will fall from the sky, and the heavenly bodies will be shaken.'	26 Men will faint from terror, apprehensive of what is coming on the world, for the heavenly bodies will be shaken.
30 At that time the sign of the Son of Man will appear in the sky, and all the nations of the earth will mourn. They will see the Son of Man coming on the clouds of the sky, with power and great glory.	26 At that time men will see the Son of Man coming in clouds with great power and glory.	27 At that time they will see the Son of Man coming in a cloud with power and great glory.
31 And he will send his angels with a loud trumpet call, and they will gather his elect from the four winds, from one end of the heavens to the other."	27 And he will send his angels and gather his elect from the four winds, from the ends of the earth to the ends of the heavens."	28 When these things begin to take place, stand up and lift up your heads, because your redemption is drawing near."

The previous discussion may provide the best solution to Matthew's "Immediately after the distress of those days ..." Is there a difference between Mark's "But in those days, following that distress (THLIPSIS)," and Matthew's "Immediately after the distress (THLIPSIS) of those days"? There may very well be!

The expression "those days" seems to point to the time that would begin *after* Jerusalem fell. It is introduced by the word TOTE in Matthew and Mark, best translated as "then," meaning "afterwards," not "at that time." In the parallel account in Luke's Gospel we find this period of "those days" described as: "Jerusalem will be trampled on by the Gentiles until the times of Gentiles are fulfilled" (Luke 21:24). As noted earlier, the term THLIPSIS, "tribulation" (*NIV* "distress"), can refer to a number of things. It describes what the church can experience in persecution, and it also refers to judgement inflicted by God upon evildoers (e.g., "the great tribulation" that the false prophetess at Thyatira, "Jezebel," and her followers would suffer–Revelation 2:22). If my understanding of "those days" is on target, then any serious problem with the sense of "immediately" disappears. Jesus referred to both the fall of Jerusalem and the subsequent opposition to His disciples as THLIPSIS. In Mark, "those days" of distress for the Christians would follow "that distress" – the destruction of Jerusalem. At some undetermined point "in those days," the signs (not warning signs!) accompanying the coming of the Son of Man would dramatically unfold in the heavens.

In Matthew, the picture of opposition described earlier in 24:23-26 is now described as "the distress of those days." No signs to signal the Lord's return would now be given. "Keep watch!" Is the exhortation. Christ's return would "immediately" follow those days. Even if "those days" are held to be the A.D. 70 tribulations, and not events following, it is clear from EUTHEOS that no intervening signs are to be expected.

The parable of the fig tree that follows (Matthew 24:32-35; Mark 13: 28-31; Luke 21:29-33) was treated in the previous chapter. Several reasons were given to include it in the section regarding the fall of Jerusalem. First, it is stylistically set apart as a distinct parable or "lesson." Second, it shows a definite emphasis on warning signs. Third, it directly relates to the near time-frame of "this generation." It clearly was not a part of Jesus' teaching concerning His Second Coming.

Matthew 24	Mark 13	Luke 21
36 "No one knows about that day or hour, not even the angels in heaven, nor the Son, but only the Father. 37 As it was in the days of Noah, so it will be at the coming of the Son of Man. 38 For in the days before the flood, people were eating and drinking, marrying and giving in marriage, up to the day Noah entered the ark; 39 and they knew nothing about what would happen until the flood came and took them all away. That is how it will be at the coming of the Son of Man. 40 Two men will be in the field; one will be taken and the other left. 41 Two women will be grinding with a hand mill; one will be taken and the other left. 42 Therefore keep watch, because you do not know on what day your Lord will come. 43 But understand this: If the owner of the house had known at what time of night the thief was coming, he would have kept watch and would not have let his house be broken into. 44 So you also must be ready, because the Son of Man will come at an hour when you do not expect him."	32 "No one knows about that day or hour, not even the angels in heaven, nor the Son, but only the Father. 33 Be on guard! Be alert! You do not know when that time will come. 34 It's like a man going away: He leaves his house and puts his servants in charge, each with his assigned task, and tells the one at the door to keep watch. 35 Therefore keep watch because you do not know when the owner of the house will come back– whether in the evening, or at midnight, or when the rooster crows, or at dawn. 36 If he comes suddenly, do not let him find you sleeping. 37 What I say to you, I say to everyone: 'Watch!'"	34 "Be careful, or your hearts will be weighed down with dissipation, drunkenness and the anxieties of life, and that day will close on you unexpectedly like a trap. 35 For it will come upon all those who live on the face of the whole earth. 36 Be always on the watch, and pray that you may be able to escape all that is about to happen, and that you may be able to stand before the Son of Man." 37 Each day Jesus was teaching at the temple, and each evening he went out to spend the night on the hill called the Mount of Olives, 38 and all the people came early in the morning to hear him at the temple.

Who Gets Left Behind?

As in the days before the flood ... eating, drinking, marrying ... the flood came and took (AIRO) them all away. That's how it will be when Jesus returns. Two men in the field, two women grinding at the mill .... In each case, one **taken** and the other **left behind**. "Left behind"! Sound familiar? Most people associate that expression with those, who, acccording to the Rapture Theory, will be left behind on earth to face the Tribulation period following the Rapture of the church. Would it surprise you that this is NOT what Rapturists teach? They can't teach it because it's not what the Bible says.

I find it ironic that the only instances in Scripture where the "taken-left behind" language is used are in texts in which the Rapturists must contend that the **Second Coming** ("Revelation") is being discussed, not the **Rapture**! (here in Matthew 24:40-41 and in Luke 17:34-36) Not only that, it's not the righteous who are taken, but the wicked! This is how it is stated regarding Noah's day. **The wicked are taken away.** It is true that two different Greek words for "taken" are used here, but the sense seems to be the same. In his discussion of Matthew 24, the dispensational scholar Stanley D. Toussaint surprisingly states, "Consistent pretribula-tionists interpret the 'taking' in these verse as a removal for judgement. The context clearly supports this meaning."[1] Are we clear on this? *The more careful Rapturists teach that the "left behind" texts are not talking about the Rapture at all, and that those left behind are actually the righteous, not the wicked!* Are you following?

Actually, in view of the variety of Second Coming and judgement scenes in the Gospels, I personally am more comfortable stating that the emphasis is on separation, not on which one is "taken" or "left behind." In the kingdom parables in Matthew 13, the variety in descriptions is readily observable. (Rapturists struggle with these—some, they believe, refer to the post-Rapture believers, others to the pre-Rapture church [!]). In the "Wheat and Tares," 13:24-30, the tares (the "wicked") are gathered up first and burned. In the "Dragnet" parable, 13:47-48, the good fish

---

[1] Stanley D. Toussaint, "Are the Church and the Rapture in Matthew 24?", in *The Return*, Thomas Ice and Timothy J. Demy, editors (Kregel Publications, 1999), p. 131.

are gathered into vessels and the bad thrown out. The latter parable describes the basic act of separation, as do the immediately following verses: "This is how it will be at the end of the age. The angels will come and separate the wicked from the righteous ..." (Matthew 13:49).

The A-B-A-B Pattern

Back to the heart of the matter. In view of the clear distinction Jesus makes between (A) A.D. 70, that which would come within that generation and would be accompanied by warning signs, and (B) the Second Coming, the event that would signal the end of the age and would be without warning, it becomes easier to show the breakdown of the Olivet Discourse. There is a non-sequential A-B-A-B pattern marked by the contrast between that which looms on the horizon and comes with warning signals, and that which will come after that important event, and will not be heralded by signs or warnings. "Be ready!" is all Jesus would advise for the latter event. The pattern is as follows:

> A. Events leading up to and including the fall of Jerusalem; clear signs given (Matthew 24:2-22; Mark 13:2-20; Luke 21:6-24a)
>
> > B. *The glorious coming of the Son of Man with power and with His holy angels. It will be sudden, immediately evident to all. (Matthew 24:23-31; Mark 13:21-27; Luke 21:24b-28)*
>
> A. The parable of the fig tree and the analogy of spring's signaling of summer; the time frame of a single generation before the fall of Jerusalem (Matthew 24:32-35; Mark 13:28-31; Luke 21:29-33)
>
> > B. *The unexpected return of the Son of Man; no one knows the day or hour; He will come like a thief in the night. (Matthew 24:36ff; Mark 13:32-37; Luke 21:34-38)*

The contrast between "A", the descriptions of the impending doom of Jerusalem, and "B", the subsequent return of the Lord, is dramatic. Even though the parable of the fig tree interrupts the sections dealing with the Second Coming, its content and tone make clear that it deals with the destruction of Jerusalem. Once that it recognized, the confusion of many over the progression of topics and images in the Olivet Discourse mostly dissipates.

Whose Glasses Are You Wearing?
Final Thoughts on the Olivet Discourse

This analysis began with a statement of the importance of this portion of Scripture. Much of the framework of the Rapture System is tied into an end-times interpretation for the "abomination of desolation" and "great tribulation" language in Matthew 24. I have invited the reader to compare Matthew, Mark and Luke to see if such an approach can be defended. In my view it is totally unjustified and a hindrance to any hope of correctly understanding Jesus' message to His disciples. An alternative interpretation has been laid out before you. It makes sense of the text, the historical context, and the known first-century fulfillment. Several options for the sense of "immediately" in Matthew were offered, and, in my view, are sufficiently reasonable, so that neither the Rapturist nor the preterist views need be sought. The A-B-A-B pattern makes sense when the key contrast is recognized– events accompanied by clear warning signs as opposed to events of which "not even the Son of Man knows the day or hour." Acceptance of this pattern clears up much of the confusion that people have about this text.

Your decision concerning the Olivet Discourse will have a major bearing on your entire millennial approach. Choose wisely.

10

THE GOLDEN AGE

"The wolf and the lamb will feed together, and the lion will eat straw like the ox, but dust will be the serpent's food. They will neither harm nor destroy on all my holy mountain," says the LORD. (Isaiah 65:25)

The prophets of ancient Israel heralded the future manifestation of a Golden Age for the people of God. Life as they then knew it would be gloriously transformed as they shared God's blessing and presence in a way they never had previously. Peace and prosperity would be the endless theme. Two questions, however, immediately surface: *when* will the Golden Age be and *who* will share in it? We believe that the Bible clearly answers both questions with answers that are quite different from the popular views today.

There are basically two approaches that can be pursued regarding the above verse in Isaiah and other related passages. The more popular approach today is to equate such descriptions with the future earthly millennium championed by dispensational premillennialists. There, according to John F. Walvoord (*The Millennial Kingdom*, p. 318), "the wolf and the lamb will feed together" *in the millennium*, indicating that at that time "the curse which creation has endured since Adam's sin will be in part suspended as even animal creation will be changed." The other distinct approach, that which we hope to demonstrate is far more Biblical, is that the Golden Age describes the Eternal State itself, a time when truly "no longer will there be any curse" (Revelation 22:3). The present world order will be replaced by a far more glorious existence on God's "new earth." Which then is it: the "millennium" or the "new heaven and new earth"? The evidence to be given now seeks to prove the latter.

Isaiah 65	Revelation 21
17 Behold, I will create new heavens and a new earth. The former things will not be remembered, nor will they come to mind.	1 Then I saw a new heaven and a new earth, for the first heaven and the first earth had passed away, and there was no longer any sea.
18 But be glad and rejoice forever in what I will create, for I will create Jerusalem to be a delight and its people a joy.	2 I saw the Holy City, the new Jerusalem, coming down out of heaven from God, prepared as a bride beautifully dressed for her husband.
19 I will rejoice over Jerusalem and take delight in my people; the sound of weeping and of crying will be heard in it no more.	4 He will wipe every tear from their eyes. There will be no more death or mourning or crying or pain, for the old order of things has passed away.

Can there be any doubt that the very things John saw are also what Isaiah predicted God would create? For further evidence that this indeed is the correct approach, note the chapter "The New Heaven and the New Earth (I)" to see the comparison between the descriptions of the "New Jerusalem" found in Isaiah 60 and Revelation 21-22.

Heaven on Earth

The remaining verses in Isaiah 65 continue to describe the future blessing in God's New Jerusalem. But here controversy develops. The descriptions Isaiah gives are very "physical" or "earthly" sounding and do not seem to match exactly what the New Testament describes. But this is not a problem. The key to the language we are about to note is that the Old Testament prophet is describing God's "new creation" in terms of "ideal existence" as the ancient Hebrews would have envisioned it. A key element is the "reversal of fortune" or freedom from invasion and captivity that plagued Israel in Isaiah's time. An analysis of the remaining verses should paint the picture clearly.

Live Long and Prosper

(20) Never again will there be in it an infant who lives but a few days, or an old man who does not live out his years; he who dies at a hundred will be thought a mere youth, he who fails to reach a hundred will be considered accursed.

Throughout the Old Testament, long life is viewed as God's blessing (Deuteronomy 6:2; 22:7; 1 Kings 3:14; Psalm 91:16; Proverbs 3:16). In the new age to come, life spans will be incredible. The hundred-year-old will be but a babe! Since no one will actually *be* "accursed" in the New Jerusalem, not one will fail to reach age one hundred. It's just the starting point.

Some might be puzzled as to how this description could be the Eternal State when it talks about people dying! The answer lies in the figurative nature of the description. Ideal existence is being described in terms to which Old Testament Israel could easily relate. A parallel to this is the "ideal picture" offered of life during Solomon's reign in I Kings 4: 25. "During Solomon's lifetime Judah and Israel, from Dan to Beersheba, lived in safety, each man under his own vine and fig tree." In a messianic prophecy describing the glorious future Kingdom, Zechariah 3:10 employs language reminiscent of the "ideal" Solomon age: "'In that day each of you will invite his neighbor to sit under his vine and fig tree,' declares the Lord Almighty." The known is used to portray the unknown.

In Isaiah, the "ideal picture" given is in stark contrast to the ordeals which Israel as a nation was facing. The message is clear that in God's future plans for His people, they need never again fear the horrors of foreign invasion and massacre.

Death's Sting Gone

Death will no longer be *premature*. But there's more. The picture presented is that death need not be feared at all. The picture far transcends the "ideal" *known* existence. Technically speaking, death is really not in the scene depicted by Isaiah. The Hebrew says literally: "For the youth will die at the age of a hundred." Since in fact no "youths" will die in the New Jerusalem, this statement is purely hypothetical. If one *were* to die at age one hundred, he or she would be but a child. In similar fashion, since no one will ever be "accursed" in the new city, no one will fail to reach the age of a hundred. Age one hundred, far beyond any reasonably hoped-for life span in Isaiah's day, will just be the *starting point* in the New Heaven and New Earth. Clearly the language of Isaiah does not stress limitation of life but the *absence of limitation*. The emphasis is not upon death, but upon abundant life.

Significantly, the parallel to Isaiah's "the sound of weeping and of crying will be heard in it no more" (65:19) found in Revelation 21:4 adds the reason why: "There will be no more death ...." (See also Isaiah 25:7-8.)

Work in Heaven?

Verses 21-23 add:

> They will build houses and dwell in them; they will plant vineyards and eat their fruit. No longer will they build houses and others live in them, or plant and others eat. For as the days of a tree, so will be the days of my people; my chosen ones will long enjoy the works of their hands. They will not toil in vain or bear children doomed to misfortune; for they will be a people blessed by the LORD, they and their descendants with them.

What about all this reference to "building and planting"? Do you mean there will be *work* in heaven? Well, in a sense there could be! Certainly the idea of sitting around playing harps all day is not real appealing, is it? "Ideal life" in the mind of the ancient Jews was not the idea of idleness, but of satisfying work.

However, the key involved here is the *reversal* of such curses as found in Deuteronomy 28:30 concerning the threat of invasion and captivity: "You will build a house, but you will not live in it. You will plant a vineyard, but you will not even begin to enjoy its fruit." The absence of death will be accompanied by the absence of calamity, loss and misfortune. (Tim LaHaye argues from this passage that there will be universal home ownership in the Millennium!)

Maternity in Eternity?

It is in this same context of building and planting that the reference to "bearing children" must be understand. Does this indicate that there is "maternity in eternity"? Not really! Rather, the contrast from the horrors of seeing innocent children slaughtered in warfare is being made. Deuteronomy predicts the further atrocities that would accompany siege (28:53-57), atrocities fulfilled in Babylon's capture of Jerusalem (Lamentations 2:

20; 4:10). To be specific, loving mothers, half-crazed by starvation, would eat their own children! The references to "not bearing children doomed to misfortune" and to "their descendants" should be viewed as ideal symbolism, not as literal. Peace, not war, will be the eternal theme.

This, by the way, is the main premillennial proof text for the idea that babies will be born during the Millennium. Parallels with the language in Revelation 21-22 indicate that we are viewing here an eternal, not a millennial, state.

(Many mistakenly find the fulfillment of Deuteronomy 28's curses above in the A.D. 70 fall to Rome. The 586 B.C. fall to Babylon is still in view there, however. Read the text carefully in comparison with the language of Leviticus 26. This is a critical point since a *regathering* from that dispersion is promised to Israel. I find no clear evidence in Scripture for a regathering of Israel following the A.D. 70 dispersion.)

Kept in Perfect Peace

> (24) "Before they call I will answer; while they are still speaking I will hear. (25) The wolf and the lamb will feed together, and the lion will eat straw like the ox, but dust will be the serpent's food. They will neither harm nor destroy on all my holy mountain," says the LORD.

The perfect prosperity and peace of the New Jerusalem will be enhanced by God's presence and intimate communication. In that city there will be no need of a sanctuary, for God Himself will be the temple (Revelation 21:22). The imagery of peace is further highlighted by the reference to the animal kingdom–natural predators along with their prey will dwell in mutual security and bliss. Truly the "curse" will be removed! Paradise will be restored.

The View of Desperationalism

All does not seem to be "well in Paradise," however. Many interpreters are forced to reject the entire approach given above. Because of an improper and inconsistent insistence upon literalism, the typical dispensational scholar cannot accept that Isaiah's language is actually a description of the Eternal State. One can certainly appreciate that concern. Terminology identical or similar to what Isaiah here employs is claimed by the premillennial camp as referring to the *millennial* earth. If our interpretation is correct, Isaiah 65's references to "building and planting," "the wolf and the lamb," etc., are indeed a figurative description of the eternal New Heaven and New Earth. Should not similar language *elsewhere* in the Old Testament then be expected to refer to the same ultimate fulfillment? If Isaiah's words here describe heaven, then what Old Testament "paradise" terminology must refer to a future "millennial earth"? In effect, the premillennialist's rationale for a "Millennium" is seriously weakened.

The dispensational solution to the problem is at best desperate. It has been referred to earlier as the "scissors and paste" method. Here is a graphic case in point. Since Isaiah's words *cannot* be referring to the Eternal State (due to dispensationalism's literalistic standards), it is argued that there must be a *break in* the passage. Verse 17 is divorced from the remaining verses 18-25. Thus, for example, C. I. Scofield (*Scofield Reference Bible*, p. 769) states: "Verse 17 looks beyond the kingdom-age to the new heavens and new earth, but verses 18-25 describe the kingdom-age itself." In the *New Scofield Bible*, the heading above verse 17 reads, "New heavens and new earth." Over verses 18-25 however, it reads, "Millennial conditions in the renewed earth with curse removed." The approach of Walvoord and Pentecost is the same in their writings. This serves as another example of "rightly dividing the Word of Truth" dispensational-style.

A careful look at the passage in question, however, should convince the unbiased reader that no break in the passage can be maintained. To argue that the verses *following* the mention of creation of the new heavens and new earth are in fact descriptions of "millennial" life *before* that very creation is folly. It is based upon an attempt to salvage the notions of a pre-conceived system, not upon sound principles of exegesis. In the words of Anthony A. Hoekema: "One will see a millennium here only if he has previously put on his millennial glasses!" (*The Meaning of the Millennium*, Robert G. Clouse, editor, p. 176)

What about the "break" with mt 24

A Closing Glimpse of Eternity

The last several verses of the book of Isaiah describe "the new heavens and new earth" from both its bright and dark sides. The glories of living in the New Jerusalem (66:10-14a) are in bold relief with the terrors for those awaiting God's fearful judgment (66:14b-17). The gathering of all nations to "my holy mountain in Jerusalem" should be equated with the description in Revelation 21:24, "the nations will walk by its light, and the kings of the earth will bring their splendor into it." The concluding words of Isaiah 66:22-24 state:

> "As the new heavens and the new earth that I make will endure before me," declares the LORD, "so will your name and descendants endure. From one New Moon to another and from one Sabbath to another, all mankind will come and bow down before me," says the LORD. "And they will go out and look upon the dead bodies of those who rebelled against me; their worm will not die, nor will their fire be quenched, and they will be loathsome to all mankind."

Here the blessed future existence of God's people is compared with the eternal duration of the new heavens and new earth. In contrast, however, we seem to find here a figurative portrayal of the utter ruin of the unrighteous (see also Malachi 4:23). The "unquenchable fire" consuming the dead bodies is best viewed as an Old Testament equivalent to Gehenna or the lake of fire.

This loathsome condition of God's enemies will never end. The references to "New Moons" and "Sabbaths" must necessarily be viewed as figurative language. Since the procedures described will continue throughout the duration of the New Heaven and New Earth, and since in the New Heaven and New Earth there will be no sun or moon (Isaiah 60:19-21; Revelation 21:23; 22:5), there obviously will no longer literally be "New Moons" and "Sabbaths." Reference to regular periodic activities such as these is employed to speak of the eternal worship of God in terms of past known practices. If time is somehow regulated, it won't be by the moon.

The symbolism in this passage rivals that found in Isaiah 65:17-25, but there is no doubt as to what each refers. Language incorporated elsewhere in the Old Testament is parallel to that found in these passages (e.g. Isaiah 11:6-9; 25:6-12; Amos 9:13-15). If this language is viewed as also describing the Eternal State, then it becomes clear that the Old Testament was a lot more "heavenly minded" than some like to think!

In light of the conspicuous absence of a "thousand-year" limitation in such passages, it would seem that a more reasonable course to take would be to view the "Golden Age" of Old Testament prophecy as referring to the same glorious age described in Revelation 21–the New Heaven and New Earth. This conclusion is based upon allowing Scripture to interpret Scripture, not upon a false standard of literalism. The "earthly" language of Isaiah 65:17-25 must not divert one away from the fact that it is indeed a portrayal of life in the "new heavens and new earth," and, as such, is a figurative description of the Eternal State. There is no Millennium to be found here.

11

THE NEW HEAVEN AND THE NEW EARTH (I)

The last two chapters in the Bible, Revelation 21-22, give us a glorious description of the Eternal State of the redeemed. The evidence given in this chapter helps support the conclusions of the previous ("The Golden Age"). The book of Revelation utilizes the Old Testament, especially Isaiah, in its description of the Eternal State, God's New Heaven and New Earth.

For many students of prophecy, Revelation 20, which contains the description of the "Millennium," is frequently the starting point for their end-times study. We believe that they are off the mark by just one chapter. But that slight miscalculation, unfortunately, has enormous repercussions.

Picking The Right Place To Start

Revelation 20 is the *wrong* place to begin an end-times study, for several reasons. First, it contains highly symbolic language that should be interpreted in light of clearer passages. Second, as explained earlier ("The Millennial Maze"), there is no agreed-upon interpretation of when and where the one-thousand year reign of Christ and his saints occurs. Is it present or future? Does it occur on earth or in heaven? Using standards of extreme literalism, some have arrived at a complex picture of the "Millennium" into which they awkwardly have forced other passages to fit. Third, a big problem is the lack of exact parallels from the Old Testament. Israel is not mentioned. The only thing that jumps out is the mention of Gog and Magog, but even that is a problem. The Rapture System teaches that this Gog and Magog invasion is *not* the same as that in Ezekiel 38-39 (see "Agog over Gog and Magog").

Revelation 21, on the other hand, is the ideal place to begin. It is true that this description of the New Heaven and New Earth contains numerous symbols and figures of speech. Consequently, the basic principle for interpreting Scripture that states in effect that we should proceed from the non-symbolic to the symbolic seems to be violated. However, what makes Revelation 21 so ideal is that virtually everyone agrees regarding what it describes. Revelation 21 is a picture of the Eternal State, using figurative language to describe spiritual realities in terms of earthly entities. The value of the passage becomes apparent. It serves as a kind of "control text." Since such symbolic language is clearly used to describe the Eternal State in this passage, when identical or even similar language is used elsewhere, it should be viewed as also referring to the Eternal State, unless compelling evidence dictates otherwise.

Descriptions of the New Jerusalem

Specific insights can be gained by noting parallels found in the Old Testament prophets. Furnished here is a convenient comparison between the language of Revelation 21-22 and Isaiah 60 in describing the future glory of "Jerusalem." You decide whether or not they are talking about the same thing!

Revelation 21-22	Isaiah 60
The city does not need the sun or the moon to shine on it, for the glory of God gives it light, and the Lamb is its lamp. (Revelation 21:23)	The sun will no more be your light by day, nor will the brightness of the moon shine on you, for the LORD will be your everlasting light, and your God will be your glory. (Isaiah 60:19)
The nations will walk by its light, and the kings of the earth will bring their splendor into it. (Revelation 21:24)	Nations will come to your light, and kings to the brightness of your dawn. (Isaiah 60:3)
On no day will its gates ever be shut, for there will be no night there. The glory and honor of the nations will be brought into it. (Revelation 21:25-26)	Your gates will always stand open, they will never be shut, day or night, so that men may bring you the wealth of the nations–their kings led in triumphal procession. (Isaiah 60:11)
There will be no more night. They will not need the light of a lamp or the light of the sun, for the Lord God will give them light. And they will reign for ever and ever. (Revelation 22:5)	Your sun will never set again, and your moon will wane no more; the LORD will be your everlasting light, and your days of sorrow will end. Then will all your people be righteous and they will possess the land forever. (Isaiah 60:20-21a)

First impressions would suggest that since Revelation's language is a description of the eternal New Jerusalem that will exist in the New Heaven and New Earth, then the language of Isaiah depicts the same. We are convinced that such is precisely the case. Isaiah is describing the eternal existence of God's people. *Who could possibly disagree?* Well, unfortunately, lots of people.

Most writers of premillennial (and particularly dispensational) persuasion are compelled to disagree because of their insistence upon the hyperliteral interpretation of certain passages. They would accordingly relegate such descriptions as found in Isaiah to a supposed future Millennial Kingdom. This alleged kingdom will be earthly and will feature the nation of Israel in the spotlight role. The insistence of these writers to take any and all prophecies concerning "Israel" as absolutely literal (perhaps "material" is a better word) causes them to ignore the obvious parallels developed above.

Of course, they themselves cannot be consistently literal regarding such promises. Even the term "forever" is qualified by them. By any literal counting method, a thousand years is not "forever." Their notion that the millennial earth will just transition into the "eternal earth" (the New Heaven and New Earth) seems incorrect in light of 2 Peter 3:10. "But the day of the Lord will come like a thief. The heavens will disappear with a roar; the elements will be destroyed by fire, and the earth and everything in it will be laid bare." So much for the old earth–millennial or otherwise.

Prominent dispensational spokesman John F. Walvoord, in his book *The Millennial Kingdom*, refers to Isaiah 60:1-17 as a description of "the lesser role of Gentiles in the millennium" (p. 303) and to Isaiah 60:21 as describing the righteousness to be manifested "in the millennial reign of Christ" (p. 307). In a book comprising over three hundred pages, he reserves his description of the New Heaven and New Earth for the last *two* pages of the book! His loaded statement that "very little description is given of this in Scripture" indicates that he would not visualize *any* connection with Isaiah 60 as offered above. In his brief discussion of the New Jerusalem, *not one Old Testament passage is offered as parallel*! What's going on here? On the other hand, he spends *several hundred pages* linking numerous Old Testament prophecies with his alleged Millennial Kingdom (including a millennial Jerusalem). Much has already been presented in this book calling into question the basic approach of the Rapture System. Here then is another suspicious practice. Dispensationalists claim that amillennialists are guilty of "robbing Israel" of its prophetic place and assigning its hope to the church. I would suggest that they are instead guilty of "robbing heaven" and assigning its descriptions to an alleged thousand-year earthly kingdom.

The City of God

The focal point of Revelation's description of the New Heaven and New Earth is the New Jerusalem. A careful analysis of the images and symbols used to describe this glorious "city" reveals a number of unique and exciting concepts to be found. Your understanding of how God's Word paints pictures through symbols and figures will be enhanced as a result of our brief journey through this passage.

Of the People, By the People, and For the People

One fascinating aspect of the usage of "city" imagery here is that two pictures are actually being developed. One picture is that of an actual city into which people enter–a city of walls, gates, and streets (21:12-26). But the other picture presented is that the city actually is the redeemed people of God. The New Jerusalem coming down out of heaven from God is, in fact, introduced twice, the second time apparently from a closer vantage point (21:2, 9-10). In both cases the first word used to describe the city is the term "bride." Compare:

> I saw the Holy City, the new Jerusalem, coming down out of heaven from God, prepared as a bride beautifully dressed for her husband (21:2).

> One of the seven angels who had the seven bowls full of the seven last plagues came and said to me, "Come, I will show you the bride, the wife of the Lamb." And he carried me away in the Spirit to a mountain great and high, and showed me the Holy City, Jerusalem, coming down out of heaven from God (21:9-10).

Scripture elsewhere identifies the Church as the bride of Christ (Ephesians 5:32). Revelation 19 earlier describes the marriage of the Lamb:

> Then I heard what sounded like a great multitude, like the roar of rushing waters and like loud peals of thunder, shouting: "Hallelujah! For our Lord God Almighty reigns. Let us rejoice and be glad and give him glory! For the wedding of the Lamb has come, and his bride has made herself ready. Fine linen, bright and clean, was given her to wear." (Fine linen stands for the righteous acts of the saints.) Then the angel said to me, "Write: 'Blessed are those who are invited to the wedding supper of the Lamb!'" And he added, "These are the true words of God." (Revelation 19:6-9)

The New Jerusalem, therefore, *is* the wife of the Lamb, the redeemed saints "clothed in fine linen" (19:8). Further elements in the imagery reinforce this people-city equation. The walls of the city contain twelve gates, each gate having the name of one of the twelve tribes of Israel written on it (21:12). The walls also have twelve foundations upon which are the names of the twelve apostles of the Lamb (21:14). The combination of Israel's tribes and Christ's apostles is a valid way to describe the totality of God's people, both Old and New Testament saints. A temple structure is replaced by the personal presence of God Himself (21:23). People and fellowship replace buildings and property in the eternal city of God (21: 3).

The absence of night enables the city gates to be open "round the clock" (21:25), a picture of peace and security (cf. Nehemiah 7:3). The striking reference, "and there was no longer any sea" (21:1), seems to signal the elimination of that which was dark, dangerous, mysterious, and foreboding (especially in light of the earlier mention in 20:13-14 of the sea "giving up its dead").

Heaven's Cube

The nature of the city and its wall is to be viewed as clearly symbolic. The dimensions of the city are those of a perfect cube, being twelve thousand stadia (equivalent to about fifteen hundred miles) in length, width, and height. Imagine the Israelis trying to put *that* settlement on the West Bank! The picture is one of strength and perfection. Very possibly the imagery is based on the Holy of Holies in the former Jerusalem temple which was also a perfect cube. Now the entire city is most holy ground! To imagine a literal cube-shaped community would be to miss the entire point, in my estimation. This would also be true of the symbolic nature of the thickness of the walls—one hundred forty-four cubits (about seventy-two yards). The use of symbolic numbers serves to strengthen the idea of perfection. (Some have suggested instead a pyramid or mountain, rather than a cube, with God's throne at the pinnacle. Either way, symbolic language is operating here.)

The city's measurements are twelve times a thousand while the walls are twelve times twelve. The numbers themselves are more significant than the units of measurement (e.g., stadia, cubits). "Twelve" seems to serve as a number of completeness just as the number "seven" more frequently does in Scripture. In light of the fact that there were twelve sons of Jacob, twelve tribes of Israel, and twelve apostles of Christ, some view twelve as being linked with God's purposes of election. Also, the Hebrew year was divided into twelve months and a day into twelve hours (note in addition the following occurrences of "twelve" in the Gospels: Matthew 14: 20; 26:53; Luke 2:42; 8:42; John 11:9). Elsewhere in Revelation, a woman (symbolizing the people of God) is pictured with a crown of twelve stars on her head (12:1). The number of those "sealed" is one hundred forty-four thousand (twelve times twelve times a thousand–"thousand" being an indefinitely large number–7:4). The tree of life in the eternal paradise of God bears twelve kinds (or "crops"–NIV) of fruit, yielding them on a monthly basis (22:2).

(*The New American Standard Bible* makes the mistake here of trying to render symbolic numbers by modern equivalents. A *stadion* was approximately six hundred feet; a *cubit* roughly a half yard. Thus "twelve thousand stadia" becomes "fifteen hundred miles" and "one hundred forty-four cubits" becomes "seventy-two yards." While such equivalence may at times be useful and desirable in modern translations, here it destroys the significance of the measurements. The actual distance is not the crucial thing, the impression left by the symbolic numbers is.)

Paradise Regained

A final glimpse within the heavenly city reveals the existence of the garden of God–Paradise regained. The amazing unity of the Bible can be clearly seen in this instance. While the early chapters of Genesis record man's banishment from Eden and his separation from the tree of life, Revelation's last chapter pictures man's complete restoration to fellowship with God. The tree of life, the leaves of which are for "the healing of the nations," is in full view, positioned next to a river of the water of life flowing down from God's throne (22:1-2; Ezekiel 47:12). The "curse" will be forever removed (22:3). Eternal life, light, and joy will be their lot. But perhaps the most glorious promise of all is found in the simple statement (22:4), "They will see his face ...."

Rapture Woe #10

Descriptions of the eternal New Jerusalem in the Old Testament are claimed by dispensationalists to refer instead to the "millennial" city, in spite of clear parallels with the eternal city of Revelation 21-22. The Rapturist claim to the normal, natural meaning of words does not always stand up under careful investigation. Terminology in the Old Testament that the Rapture System claims for the Millennium is the same used in the New for the Eternal State.

12

THE N   HEAVEN AND THE
EARTH (II)

> But the day of the Lord will come like a thief. The heavens will disappear with a roar; the elements will be destroyed by fire, and the earth and everything in it will be laid bare. Since everything will be destroyed in this way, what kind of people ought you to be? You ought to live holy and godly lives as you look forward to the day of God and speed its coming. That day will bring about the destruction of the heavens by fire, and the elements will melt in the heat. But in keeping with his promise we are looking forward to a new heaven and a new earth, the home of righteousness. (2 Peter 3:10-13)

The glorious return of Jesus Christ, described throughout Scripture as "the day of the Lord," will usher in the New Heaven and New Earth. The above description found in 2 Peter 3 shows that our Lord's return will spell the end of the present world order. In spite of this clear teaching, confusion remains for some regarding several key related subjects. What exactly does the Bible mean by "heaven," and is that where we go when we die? Just how "physical" will the "new creation" be? Are Paradise and heaven the same thing? What about Hades and hell? Is eternal life something we wait for or something we already possess? Our attempts to answer these and similar questions will be brief, but they are essential to grasp for a proper understanding of God's present and future plans.

Heaven: Old and New

An initial hurdle to overcome involves the very word "heaven." What does Peter mean when he writes that "the heavens will disappear with a roar" (2 Peter 3:10)? In Scripture the term "heaven" or "the heavens" can mean several things: (1) the sky or atmosphere; (2) what we would refer to as "outer space"; and (3) the realm or place of God's full presence, i.e., the spirit realm. It is the last meaning that most rightly think of when the word "heaven" is used in the Bible.

It is clear, however, that in the expression "New Heaven and New Earth" the word "Heaven" is to be thought of in the sense of sky or space. "Heaven and New Earth" becomes a phrase to describe the entire universe, the totality of physical existence. "A New Heaven and New Earth," then, means a *new creation*.

Peter says that both the present heavens and earth will be destroyed or dissolved (and they will be replaced by a new heaven and a new earth). John in Revelation says something similar: "Then I saw a great white throne and him who was seated on it. Earth and sky (lit. "heaven") fled from his presence, and there was no place for them" (Revelation 20:11). He further writes, "Then I saw a new heaven and a new earth, for the first heaven and the first earth had passed away, and there was no longer any sea" (21:1) ... "for the old order of things has passed away" (21:4).

When people speak of "heaven" as referring to the eternal dwelling place of God's people, they are actually referring to what the Bible describes as "the New Heaven and New Earth." This state of existence will differ from the present order in that God's presence will be immediate, thus it is a more "spiritual" existence. God and man will be directly united in this new creation.

How "Physical" Will the New Creation Be?

Because of the differing images presented in Scripture, the exact nature or make-up of the new heaven and earth is debated. The language of 2 Peter 3 could be interpreted as either a renovation of the present universe into a "new, improved model," or the annihilation of the physical order and the subsequent replacement of it with a spiritual or "non-material" realm. The key question seems to be: How much continuity or discontinuity should one envision between the old and new creations?

Some passages would seem to stress the continuity between old and new. Such a passage is Romans 8:19-23:

> The creation waits in eager expectation for the sons of God to be revealed. For the creation was subjected to frustration, not by its own choice, but by the will of the one who subjected it, in hope that the creation itself will be liberated from its bondage to decay and brought into the glorious freedom of the children of God. We know that the whole creation has been groaning as in the pains of childbirth right up to the present time. Not only so, but we ourselves, who have the firstfruits of the Spirit, groan inwardly as we wait eagerly for our adoption as sons, the redemption of our bodies.

This passage seems to imply renovation, i.e., the very redemption of creation, the removal of the "curse" imposed by the Fall.

On the other hand, the language of Revelation 21-22, which in fact utilizes the "Paradise-restored" theme (22:1-2) and specifically states that "there shall no longer be any curse" (22:3), makes it clear that the symbolism employed defies a strictly "material" interpretation. The "cube" imagery of the New Jerusalem should not cause one to calculate feet, yards, and acres. In the new creation, God Himself will be the light (and its lamp will be the Lamb) and the Lord God, the Almighty, and the Lamb will be its temple (21:22-23). No one would stress the "physical" or "material" nature of God's "throne" which sits in the New Jerusalem (and there is no evidence to theorize a change in thrones between Revelation 20: 11-12 and 22:1). Revelation, then seems to indicate a continuity between the present spirit realm and the future New Heaven and New Earth.

Will the New Heaven and New Earth be "physical" or "spiritual"? The Biblical picture would seem to imply both! Any valid debate can only be over the question of degree. Scientists have seemingly bridged the previous gap between "matter" and "energy." We should have no trouble viewing God as bridging the gap between "matter" and "spirit"! After all, He is the Creator of both.

One must keep in mind that something need not be "physical" in order to be real. The present environment or domain in which God personally dwells (a "dimension" parallel to ours?) is just as real as our physical universe. Our image of clouds, people floating, etc., had led to a view that heaven is a somewhat "hazy" or "airy" existence. This may miss the real case altogether. The great Christian writer C. S. Lewis, in his own provocative way, has insinuated that, after all, "spirit" may very well be *heavier* than "matter" (*Miracles*, p. 95)! In his delightful novel, *The Great Divorce*, Lewis writes from the perspective of a passenger on a bus excursion from Hell to the bright borders of Heaven. Among other discoveries, he noted that the field or plain that led up to Heaven itself was made up of much more solid stuff than he was used to. The blades of grass felt hard as diamonds. He nearly exhausted himself trying to pick up a single tiny tree leaf from the ground. He was unable to but budge the stalk of even the smallest daisy. His visit to Heaven was truly a "real" shock!

The Bible itself warns us not to be enamored by our present "real" world. The book of Hebrews informs us that the "true tabernacle" is in heaven, one "set up by the Lord, not by men" (Hebrews 8:2). The Levitical priests of Judaism served "a copy and shadow of what is in heaven" (8:5). Regarding the Old Testament blood sacrifices, Hebrews states:

> It was necessary, then, for the copies of the heavenly things to be purified with these sacrifices, but the heavenly things themselves with better sacrifices than these. For Christ did not enter a man-made sanctuary that was only a copy of the true one; he entered heaven itself, now to appear for us in God's presence. (Hebrews 9:23-24)

The New Heaven and New Earth will be a glorious reality some day. However, to insist upon its being a "physical" reality may be a mistaken preference for the "shadow" over against the "substance."

The Resurrection Body

A question that continues to crop up today also clearly plagued Paul in his day: "How are the dead raised? With what kind of body will they come?" (I Corinthians 15:35) If one's curiosity was not satisfied with our answer concerning the nature of the New Heaven and New Earth, it will probably not be satisfied with Paul's answer regarding the nature of the "new body." Paul's only recourse to this inquiry is to borrow an analogy from nature. Figurative language once again is required to illustrate a deep theological truth.

Paul notes the progression from seed to plant and compares that with the transition from physical body to spiritual (heavenly) body. The apostle writes,

> How foolish! What you sow does not come to life unless it dies. When you sow, you do not plant the body that will be, but just a seed, perhaps of wheat or of something else. But God gives it a body as he

has determined, and to each kind of seed he gives its own body. (1 Corinthians 15:36-38)

> So will it be with the resurrection of the dead. The body that is sown is perishable, it is raised imperishable; it is sown in dishonor, it is raised in glory; it is sown in weakness, it is raised in power; it is sown a natural body, it is raised a spiritual body. If there is a natural body, there is also a spiritual body. (1 Corinthians 15:42-44)

How "physical" or "spiritual" will the "resurrection body" be? Any attempt to go beyond Paul's analogy here would be misguided. One thing is certain: our "new bodies" will be perfectly tailored for a glorious existence in God's "New Heaven and New Earth."

The Intermediate State

The terminology "New Heaven and New Earth" or "Eternal State" may be new to you. Most Christians tend to (over)simplify things by merely stating that when people die they go either to heaven or hell. Such a statement can be on the hand true, but on the other misleading. In order to get a clearer picture of the Bible's teaching on this important subject, it is better to stick with specific Biblical terms and allow them to sharpen our focus as much as possible.

Paradise, Heaven, and the New Heaven and New Earth

As had already been noted, the term "heaven" can be a catch-all word with a variety of connotations. Not that we should avoid the word. It's just that we need to understand what is meant by it in various contexts. Probably the most useful distinction to be made regarding the fate of the righteous (those "in Christ") involves the two categories "Intermediate State" and "Eternal State." Once these are understood, you may then fit in the word "heaven" as you desire.

Technically speaking, the expression that the Bible itself uses to describe the eternal or final state of the redeemed is "the New Heaven and New Earth." *Chronologically*, this Eternal State appears to come into existence only after the Second Coming of Christ (compare Revelation 19:9-21 with 20:7-21:2). Therefore, prior to Jesus' return, the New Heaven and New Earth is not yet in existence.

The term "Intermediate State" is used by some to describe the abode of the righteous dead prior to the Second Coming. Various descriptive words and phrases are employed in Scripture to elucidate the matter. On the cross, Jesus used the term "Paradise" (originally from the Persian word "garden") to describe where He and the penitent thief would that day be (Luke 23:43). "Paradise" seems to be as convenient a term as any to describe the present state of the righteous dead. The picture portrayed is one of blissful joy and comfort.

In the story of the Rich Man and Lazarus, the poor beggar Lazarus is described after death as being carried by the angels to "Abraham's bosom" (Luke 16:19-31). His lot was a far cry from the fiery torment that the rich man had to endure for his wickedness. Paul described the state of righteous bliss as simply to be "with Christ" (Philippians 1:23) or to be "at home with the Lord" (II Corinthians 5:8).

The word "heaven" could also fittingly be applied to this blessed state. In this sense when we die we *do* "go to heaven." Just as possible, however, is the use of "heaven" to describe the final state or "New Heaven and New Earth" ushered in at the Second Coming. "Heaven" in the sense of "where God is," can be used to describe both the Intermediate and Eternal States.

The relationship between the Intermediate State and Eternal State is one of both continuity and discontinuity. For those who die this side of the Second Coming, their eternal fate is forever sealed. Those in Paradise will certainly participate in the later New Creation. There exists the same finality for the wicked. A great chasm is described as fixed between the abode of Lazarus and the rich man (Luke 16:26). The blessings of Paradise merge with the glorious Eternal State. On the other hand, Scripture still indicates a *change* that will occur at the Second Coming of Christ. The redeemed will enjoy a more complete and glorious existence with the reception of their "new bodies" suited for the eternal "New Heaven and New Earth." We feel it best to stress the continuity involved but also to recognize the change.

Hades, Hell, and the Lake of Fire

The same problem unfortunately exists for the word "hell" as exists for the word "heaven." Opinions vary as to whether "hell" should be used for either the Intermediate State of the wicked or for their Final State or for both.

The Greek word HADES is the name for the abode of the dead (its Hebrew counterpart in the Old Testament is SHEOL). Its literal meaning is the "unseen" world. The ancient Greeks divided Hades into two parts: *Elysium*, the abode of the righteous, and *Tartarus*, the abode of the wicked. This distinction, however, is not explicitly maintained in the New Testament. The term Hades is found eleven times in the New Testament (Matthew 11:23; 16:18; Luke 10:15; 16:23; Acts 2:27, 31; I Corinthians 15:55; Revelation 1:18; 6:8; 20:13-14). It connotes a *negative* idea. Christians are *never* said to "go to Hades" at death.

Hades apparently then is utilized in the New Testament to describe the abode of the *unrighteous* dead (the concept of "Tartarus" is referred to once in II Peter 2:4 by using the verb TARTARAO–God has "tartarized" fallen angels, holding them for the final judgment).

The English word "hell" is a translation of the Greek word GE HEN-NA (The King James Version has unfortunately rendered Hades as "hell" also, causing considerable confusion). Gehenna occurs twelve times, eleven times used by Jesus (Matthew 5:22, 29, 30; 10:28; 18:9; 23:15, 33; Mark 9:43, 45, 47; Luke 12:5) and once in James 3:6. Gehenna is the Greek equivalent of the Hebrew GE HINNOM, "valley of Hinnom." The Valley of Hinnom, bordering Jerusalem on the southeast, was used in earlier times for the idolatrous worship of pagan deities such as Baal. These rites even included the abomination of infant sacrifice. Later, the valley was used by the Jews as the refuse heap of the city. Fires burned continually in the valley to consume the garbage and waste dumped there. What a graphic word Jesus chose to describe the fate of the wicked!

Although the rich man in Hades (Luke 16:23-24) is described as also being in torment in the flames, the word "hell" might best be reserved to describe the Eternal State of the wicked, the "second death" or the "lake of fire." Whatever grief is experienced in Hades is unfortunately but a foretaste of the final condition. Just as with Paradise and the New Heaven and New Earth, so here a chronological sequence is indicated. At the time of the Second Coming and resulting Judgment Day, the unrighteous are thrown into the lake of fire (Revelation 20:15). John writes, "Then death and Hades were thrown into the lake of fire. The lake of fire is the second death" (Revelation 20:14). The fate of the wicked is fixed at physical death, contrary to what some modern-day cults may teach. The *continuity* between Hades and the lake of fire must be stressed (most generally use the term "hell" to describe the latter). We must also note, however, a *change* that occurs at the Second Coming with regard to the situation of the dead.

Living in the Future Tense

The Christian does not need to wait until the Second Coming of Christ in order to begin tasting the joys of eternal life. Eternal life should not be viewed just as a future hope, it is a *present* possession. John writes, "And this is the testimony: God has given us eternal life, and this life is in his Son. He who has the Son has life ...." (I John 5:11-12a)

Those who will share in the New Creation brought into existence at the Second Coming will be the ones who have been "created anew" by the blood of Jesus Christ. "Therefore, if anyone is in Christ, he is a new creation; the old has gone, the new has come!" (II Corinthians 5:17) In baptism we are buried with Christ into death in order to be raised to a new life (Romans 6:4).

The glorious return of Christ is indeed, as Paul puts it, our "blessed hope" (Titus 2:13). That hope, however, has definite implications for our life and lifestyle in the here and now. Paul challenges us in Colossians 3:1-4:

> Since, then, you have been raised with Christ, set your hearts on things above, where Christ is seated at the right hand of God. Set your minds on things above, not on earthly things. For you died, and your life is now hidden with Christ in God. When Christ, who is your life, appears, then you also will appear with him in glory.

Someday we will appear ("be manifested") in glory with Him, but already we are raised with Him. Already we live in Him (Colossians 2:6; Philippians 1:21; 1 John 4:9, 13). Already we are overcomers in Him (1 John 2:13-14; 4:4; 5:4).

13

AGOG OVER GOG AND MAGOG

AGOG - "full of intense interest or excitement" (Merriam-Webster)

GOG - A member of an end-times alliance that God will summons to enter into a climactic "battle," according to Ezekiel 38-39. See fact sheet below.

MAGOG - A son of Japheth (Genesis 10:2; 1 Chronicles 1:5) who teams up with Gog, Meshech, Tubal and others to annihilate God's people. It doesn't work out very well for them! See fact sheet below.

> "World politics, like the history of Gog and Magog,
> are very confused and much disputed."
> (Winston Churchill, 9 November 1951)

The is a great deal of interest in the Rapturist scheme of things over what the prophet Ezekiel refers to as the invasion of *Gog and Magog*. Taken literally (which must be done regarding all things about "Israel," remember), Ezekiel's description involves an end-times attack upon the nation of Israel, in which these foreign nations are destroyed and God's reputation is enhanced. Ezekiel 38:21-23 describes the "battle" and its results this way:

> "I will summon a sword against Gog on all my mountains," declares the Sovereign LORD. "Every man's sword will be against his brother. I will execute judgment upon him with plague and bloodshed; I will pour down torrents of rain, hailstones and burning sulfur on him and on his troops and on the many nations with him. And so I will show my greatness and my holiness, and I will make myself

known in the sight of many nations. Then they will know that I am the LORD."

Everyone Agog

From Islam's holy book, the Quran, to English mythology, the names Gog and Magog have certainly claimed their share of interest throughout history. In more recent years Muslim scholars have used the names in reference to the Christian nations of the West. Jewish interpretations (especially in the Targums–Aramaic translations of the Old Testament) ranged from Babylon, Assyria and Rome, to the Scythians, Goths, Germania, and the Christians and Turks. Later Jews saw Napoleon I and his army as the fulfillment.

A survey of Christians views through the centuries would add to the previous list the Saracens, Mongols, Tartars, Huns, Magyars, Muslims, and others.

The history of the attempts to identify Gog and Magog is a showcase of the politicization of the Bible. One's current enemies have made perfect candidates over the years for the process that Nicholas M. Railton calls "gogification." Both sides of the Civil War, e.g., claimed the identification for the other side!

Even as Gog and Magog were applied to the panorama of political and military events, many biblical commentators down through the centuries have seen an apocalyptic, end times application for the Ezekiel 38-39 account. With the scholars Jerome and Augustine in the 4th century, a shift can be seen away from the notion of political enemies to that of God's enemies or spiritual warfare. In more recent times the dispensational *Scofield Reference Bible* has tapped Russia as the eschatological enemy of God and the nation of Israel. Although the Hebrew word ROSH most likely means "head, chief," not "Russia" (e.g., as in *NIV* "chief prince") the Russia/Soviet Union prophetic bandwagon gained a sizeable following in the 70's and 80's with Rapturist interpreters like John Walvoord, Jack van Impe, Salem Kirban, Hal Lindsey, Tim LaHaye and a host others. The last several decades have shown that when premillennial prognosticators have seen their timetables and featured end-times personalities or political scenarios go up in smoke, they have been very versatile in their ability to "adjust" their predictions to fit the new circumstances and developments.[1]

What's a Gog?

The Bible offers several clues how to understand the nature of the Gog-Magog conflict. Recognizing the role of these entities in ancient times makes reasonable the view that these names play a symbolic role in Ezekiel and later in Revelation.

The Gog and Magog Fact Sheet

Here are some bits of information to help you in your understanding of Gog and Magog.

#1 Most of the names in the Gog-Magog "alliance" refer to ancient peoples of the north and west (along with the south–Cush and Put– and southeast–Sheba and Dedan).

#2 All these nations did business with the city kingdom of Tyre (Ezekiel 27).

#3 Meshech-Tubal is listed along with Assyria, Elam, Edom, Sidonians and the princes of the north, and Egypt as those lying in their graves in Sheol (Ezekiel 32). They are all slain by the sword, uncircumcised. They all at one time instilled terror in the "land of the living" (Ezekiel 32:26) but they have all met their demise.

#4 These ancient enemies seem to serve a symbolic function in Ezekiel's description of the ultimate destruction of God's enemies.

#5 They will seek to destroy God's people "after many days, at the end of years" when Israel lives in complete security, at rest, in unwalled villages" (38:8-11).

#6 Revelation 20 states that Satan will stir up Gog and Magog at the end of the "thousand years."

#7 As in the description in Revelation 20, no actual battle occurs in Ezekiel (38:18-23).

---

[1] Much of the above summary was aided by the useful article by Nicholas M. Railton, "Gog and Magog: Story of a Symbol," *Evangelical Quarterly* 75:1 (2003), 23-43.

The Master of Metaphor

Ezekiel's vision concerning Gog and Magog should be studied in light of the overall nature of Ezekiel's prophecies. I would grant the prophet Ezekiel the title "Master of Metaphor." The Bible, including its prophetic portions, is full of literary metaphors. Metaphors are transferences of meaning to other objects in ways that make our language richer. If money were water, then a rich man could "drown in his money"! Jesus described the wily Herod as a "fox." Jerusalem at times is called "Sodom" when its sinful condition is being emphasized.

Ezekiel is noteworthy for his *extended* metaphors. He prophesied in tough times to a troubled people in captivity. They are referred to as "stiff-necked" and rebellious. They had experienced gut-wrenching shock in connection with the punitive devastation of their temple and homeland. They now needed a wake-up call.

The visions God brings to light through this unique prophet are loaded with plenty of shock value themselves. Vivid scenes and narrations certainly grab the attention, and at times are not pleasant fare for the timid. The audience that had been dragged into captivity was past the prim and proper phase of existence, and had seen the worse atrocities that war and defeat can bring. Getting their attention would not be an easy thing. Modern readers may need to brace themselves.

Reading Ezekiel's painfully long, lurid, detailed description of the whoredom of the "twisted sisters" Oholah and Oholibah (Samaria and Jerusalem– Ezekiel 23) in a sermon would make any congregation squirm. Or try the three sisters–Jerusalem, Sodom, and Samaria–in Ezekiel 16. Whew! Same crowd effect.

Other metaphors cover a remarkable range of topics and expressions. The arrogant king of Tyre had been a "cherub" in the garden of Eden (Ezekiel 28), and the city of Tyre itself was a mighty sailing ship (Ezekiel 27). Egypt was a great sea monster (Ezekiel 31), and Israel was a pile of dead bones in a valley (Ezekiel 37). The garden of Eden is mentioned all over the place. Symbols from nature abound. (The recognition of the widespread use of "extended metaphor" in Ezekiel may be of some help in fathoming the unique "Temple Vision" in Ezekiel 40-48 as well. Once Ezekiel latches on to an idea, he really runs with it!)

Note Well: Any interpretation of the prophecies of Israel's "restoration" or "return" must take into account the prophet's life setting. Ezekiel preached to Israel while they were in the Babylonian captivity. So did Jeremiah. Jeremiah, Habakkuk and Zephaniah all predicted the coming of that captivity a short time before Jerusalem was destroyed in 586 B.C. Isaiah looked ahead into the distance and prophesied concerning the same captivity.

Dispensationalists often ignore this important historical setting of the prophets. The result? They take the message of restoration from captivity by these same prophets and make them apply to the modern return to the land many centuries after the Roman destruction of the temple and city. What happened to the setting of these prophecies? What happened to the return from Babylon? The restoration described in the books of Haggai, Zechariah, Ezra and Nehemiah is pretty much ignored by these interpreters.

One would think that Ezekiel had in mind a restoration from the captivity in which he and his audience were participating! Doesn't this make perfect sense? The same goes for Jeremiah's audience, etc. It must be admitted that some of the language describing this return is rather lofty, elevated, idealistic. Several reasons for this are likely. Poetic license is always a factor. Most of the prophetic message of the Old Testament was in poetic form (using parallel thoughts, not rhyming sounds). Some of the language may have been conditional, and the less than consistent faithfulness of the returnees diminished the actual fulfillment.

More importantly, however, the prophets at times blended future events together so that fulfillments were separated by significant lengths of time. For example, the Old Testament does not distinguish between the first and second comings of Christ. Elements of each can be blended into a single prophecy.

The big question for now, however, is which future event represents the first "mountain peak" that the prophets viewed. In view of the setting of most of the prophetic books, written during or before the Babylonian captivity, it must be argued that *the first mountain peak was the return from the captivity in which the prophets and their immediate audiences were involved.* Any other answer flies in the face of good sense. Whatever prophetic "blending" or "telescoping" that we may envision, the beginning of the "blend" should start with the restoration from captivity connected with the fall of Babylon, 539 B.C. This is fundamental to a proper understanding of the restoration promises in the Old Testament.

Judgement Imagery

In ancient times, God used godless nations and enemy empires to deliver his blows of punishment upon his disobedient people. Assyria (Isaiah 10:5) and Babylon (Habakkuk 1:6ff), for example, executed judgement upon Israel and Judah respectively. In the future, God will judge the entire world in righteousness and power. Sometimes that judgement is described as a great harvest, or the treading of grapes in the wine vat. Joel 3:13 says, "Swing the sickle, for the harvest is ripe. Come, trample the grapes, for the winepress is full and the vats overflow– so great is their wickedness!"

More often it is described as a great battle in which the Lord will defeat the enemy and bring them into judgement. Again in Joel we read,

> Proclaim this among the nations: Prepare for war! Rouse the warriors! Let all the fighting men draw near and attack. Beat your plowshares into swords and your pruning hooks into spears. Let the weakling say, "I am strong!" Come quickly, all you nations from every side, and assemble there. Bring down your warriors, O LORD! "Let the nations be roused; let them advance into the Valley of Jehoshaphat, for there I will sit to judge all the nations on every side."
> (Joel 3:9-12)

Often God is viewed as initiating the battle. After all, it is for His purposes in judging and punishing His enemies. These are not real battles, but rather symbols and scenes of the wrath of the Lord. The "battles" in the book of Revelation are not battles either–look at the descriptions of Armageddon (Revelation 16), the victory of the King of Kings on the white horse (Revelation 19), or Satan's Gog and Magog maneuver (Revelation 20). Victory is quick, complete, and there are no casualties for the winning side. God's enemies and the enemies of His people are overwhelmed and crushed forever. That's how the story ends. Almighty God reigns victorious forever over the redeemed.

Tim LaHaye and Thomas Ice seem to recognize this to a point. Here's their take on the description of the Revelation 19 "battle":

Note also that Jesus will come with the armies of heaven "following him, riding on white horses and dressed in fine linen, white and clean" (Revelation 19:14 *NIV*). The armies of heaven consist of the angelic hosts, the Old Testament saints, the church, and the Tribulation saints. What's especially significant is the garb of this army: They are "dressed in fine linen, white and clean." Military men are issued darker-colored uniforms for battle dress–not only for camouflage, but also because light-colored clothes would become soiled immediately. By contrast, the Commander in Chief of the heavenly forces clothes His army in white, a practice unheard of in the history of warfare. Christ will do this because no member of His army will do battle. Not one of us will lift a finger, for the battle will be carried out of by the spoken word of our Lord Himself. (*Charting the End Times*, p. 66)

Ezekiel's Gog and Magog episode serves to show that God's people will prevail. Someday every knee will bow and acknowledge the one true God.

"This is what will happen in that day: When Gog attacks the land of Israel, my hot anger will be aroused," declares the Sovereign LORD. "In my zeal and fiery wrath I declare that at that time there shall be a great earthquake in the land of Israel. The fish of the sea, the birds of the air, the beasts of the field, every creature that moves along the ground, and all the people on the face of the earth will tremble at my presence. The mountains will be overturned, the cliffs will crumble and every wall will fall to the ground. I will summon a sword against Gog on all my mountains," declares the Sovereign LORD. "Every man's sword will be against his brother. I will execute judgment upon him with plague and bloodshed; I will pour down torrents of rain, hailstones and burning sulfur on him and on his troops and on the many nations with him. And so I will show my greatness and my holiness, and I will make myself known in the sight of many nations. Then they will know that I am the LORD." (Ezekiel 38:18-23)

"Then they will know that I am the LORD."

The Problem of Gog's Timing

Some may not favor my more "figurative" approach to the Gog and Magog oracle in Ezekiel. They need to recognize the serious problems that any "literal" alternative has, however. Rapturists wrestle mightily over the exact timing when such an invasion described in Ezekiel could literally take place. Their efforts to arrive at a satisfactory solution are doomed, and the reasons for that become obvious.

Time Slot #1:
Satan's Loosing at the End of the Millennium

It might seem obvious to some (like me) that the New Testament mention of Gog and Magog at Revelation 20:8 would settle the issue, but that, alas, is not even close to being the case. We read,

> When the thousand years are over, Satan will be released from his prison and will go out to deceive the nations in the four corners of the earth–Gog and Magog– to gather them for battle. In number they are like the sand on the seashore. They marched across the breadth of the earth and surrounded the camp of God's people, the city he loves. But fire came down from heaven and devoured them.
> (Revelation 20:7-9)

This just won't work in the dispensational scheme of things, for several reasons. First, the precise connections are not sufficient for their standard of literalness. The biggest problem, however, seems to center around their literal interpretation of the time mentioned after the battle in Ezekiel. For "seven months" the bodies will be buried (39:12), and for "seven years" Gog's weapons will be burned as fuel to save Israel from having to gather or cut wood for themselves (39:9-10). How convenient! This seven-year period is a real problem for LaHaye and friends. Much time is spent wrestling over this "problem." (If one would just recognize the symbolic nature of "seven" here as a number signifying completeness, the trouble goes away.)

Obviously, if the Gog and Magog defeat ushers in the Eternal State, as it does at the end of Revelation 20, burning weapons for fuel will not really be an issue! And let the dead bury the dead. Option #1 won't work for the Rapture System. There must be *two* "Gog and Magog" pairs in Scripture, and that cannot be viewed as a good thing, can it?

Time Slot #2:
Christ's Second Coming

Coming on the white horse in Revelation 19, Christ destroys His enemies with the sword from His mouth. Now this passage looks promising as the fulfillment also. (This would make sense, since in the amillennial way of viewing things the battles in Revelation 19 and 20 are talking about the same thing.) The parallels between Revelation 19 and Ezekiel 38-39 are striking indeed.

Ezekiel 39	Revelation 19
"Son of man, this is what the Sovereign LORD says: **Call out to every kind of bird and all the wild animals: 'Assemble and come together from all around to the sacrifice I am preparing for you, the great sacrifice on the mountains of Israel. There you will eat flesh and drink blood. You will eat the flesh of mighty men and drink the blood of the princes of the earth as if they were rams and lambs, goats and bulls–all of them fattened animals from Bashan. At the sacrifice I am preparing for you, you will eat fat till you are glutted and drink blood till you are drunk. At my table you will eat your fill of horses and riders, mighty men and soldiers of every kind,' declares the Sovereign LORD.** 'I will display my glory among the nations, and all the nations will see the punishment I inflict and the hand I lay upon them.'" (Ezekiel 39:17-21)	And I saw an angel standing in the sun, who **cried in a loud voice to all the birds flying in midair, "Come, gather together for the great supper of God, so that you may eat the flesh of kings, generals, and mighty men, of horses and their riders, and the flesh of all people, free and slave, small and great."** Then I saw the beast and the kings of the earth and their armies gathered together to make war against the rider on the horse and his army. But the beast was captured, and with him the false prophet who had performed the miraculous signs on his behalf. With these signs he had deluded those who had received the mark of the beast and worshiped his image. The two of them were thrown alive into the fiery lake of burning sulfur. **The rest of them were killed with the sword that came out of the mouth of the rider on the horse, and all the birds gorged themselves on their flesh.** (Revelation 19:17-21)

These close parallels apparently won't work, for the same reasons. Those seven years just don't seem to work out here, either. No one thinks that it makes sense for Israel to be burning weapons for fuel once the Second Coming has occurred and the Millenial Kingdom kicks in (plus, you've got all those extra dead bodies now!). So this close parallel must be rejected, the Rapture System concludes.

Time Slot #3:
The Battle of Armageddon

Amillennialists believe that Armageddon is a symbolic description of the final "conflict" in connection with the Second Coming. There is ONE future dramatic, divine intervention into this present world order according to amillennialism–the Second Coming. For Rapturists, there are at least *five or so*: Gog and Magog; the Rapture; Armageddon; the Second Coming; and the Satanic Gog and Magog. Without these highly unlikely distinctions, the Rapture System disintegrates, since its hyperliteral assumptions would be violated.

Har Megiddo, "the hill of Megiddo," was a strategic battle site in ancient Palestine, much like, say, Gettysburg would be in American thought. The line of advance for armies between Egypt and Mesopotamia(Assyria, Babylon, Persia) would pass through a critical valley overlooked by the hill of Megiddo. In an age of smart bombs, nuclear weapons, stealth bombers and cruise missiles, how strategic could such a small piece of real estate be? Not very, really. But in ancient times, it was of *huge* importance. It was in this area, for example, that the great king of Judah Josiah died, when he tried to stop the advance of the Egyptian army through his land (2 Kings 23:29). The term (H)armageddon (the Greek language had no letter "H" in New Testament times) served as a symbol of a place of climactic confrontation involving the people of God.

The Rapturist understanding differs dramatically. Lahaye and Ice outline the "Eight Stages of Armageddon":

1. The assembling of the allies of the Antichrist (Psalm 2:1-6; Joel 3: 9-11; Revelation 16:12-16).

2. The destruction of Babylon (Isaiah 13-14; Jeremiah 50-51; Zechariah 5:5-11; Revelation 17-18).

3. The fall of Jerusalem (Micah 4:11-5:1; Zechariah 12-14).

4. The armies of the Antichrist at Bozah (Jeremiah 49:13-14; Micah 2:12).

5. The national regeneration of Israel (Psalm 79:1-13; 80:1-19; Isaiah 64:1-12; Hosea 6:1-13; Joel 2:28-32; Zechariah 12:10; 13:7-9; Romans 11:25-27).

6. The second coming of Jesus Christ (Isiah 34:1-7; 63:1-3; Micah 2: 12-13; Habakkuk 3:3).

7. The battle from Bozrah to the Valley of Jehoshaphat (Jeremiah 49: 20-22; Joel 3:12-13; Zechariah 14:12-15).

8. The victory ascent upon the Mount of Olives (Joel 3:14-17; Zechariah 14:3-5; Matthew 24:29-31; Revelation 16:17-21; 19:11-21).
(Charting the End Times, p. 63)

It would take another book to respond to this amazing list! One of the greatest mistakes of dispensationalists is their pulling verses out of context with alarming frequency in order to buttress their claims. Few of the Old Testament citations in this list predict the battle of Armageddon (*none* the "Armageddon" of dispensationalism). The cut-and-paste method is irresistible since it provides such impressive results, and few of the loyal followers of these gurus seem to know the difference. This is the genius of pretribulational dispensational premillennialism. It is also its downfall. Rapturists promise their following a short-cut to knowing the great wisdom of God's prophetic plan. It really doesn't take long to learn. It could be called "microwave theology." The problem with it is that the results just aren't well done.

A careful look at the above Old Testament references will make it obvious that these verses have been ripped out of their respective contexts and given a meaning or application that they were not intended to have. Start with Joel 2:28-32 (Acts 2!), Jeremiah 49, and keep going. These are not Armageddon texts, and, by the way, the purpose of the *biblical* battle of Armageddon is NOT, as Lahaye and Ice refer to it, "to gather the armies of the world to execute the Antichrist's 'final solution' to the 'Jewish problem.'" (*Charting*, p. 63) Poor wording for a poor interpretation.

Back to the "seven years" problem. Tim LaHaye believes that Armageddon is a campaign during the last part of the Great Tribulation. It is ended by the Second Coming, so there is no room for the seven years or seven months here, either. This is a frightful campaign, however, before Christ finally arrives. Babylon is destroyed. Jerusalem is destroyed. But Israel now repents! Amazing. This terrible campaign accomplishes what both the Gog and Magog deliverance and the Rapture could not! I'll say it again. Amazing.

Time Slot #4:
The Elusive Solution

The Rapturists believe that neither Revelation 20's Gog and Magog, nor Revelation 19's Second Coming, nor Revelation 16's Armageddon campaign can be the description of Ezekiel's Gog and Magog invasion. So WHEN IS IT? They wish they could tell you! That is, they wish they could give you a satisfactory answer. Again, that seven-year ditch they can't cross over.

Not This One

Two unlikely scenarios are considered by LaHaye (*Charting*, pp. 92-93). And remember, two wrong answers don't make a right! Possibly Gog and Magog takes place 3½ years *before* the Rapture and so the seven years would terminate right before the Antichrist got into full swing. All kinds of problems here, however. Would the Rapture be a surprise 3½ years after the events described in Ezekiel 38-39 took place? Hardly. Would the Rapture be "imminent" if it had to be preceded by Gog and Magog, etc.? Lots of problems.

Not This One, Either

The other answer given, then, is that the Rapture actually doesn't come seven years before the Second Coming! (Time to rewrite the dispensational textbooks, it seems). It's *Antichrist's signing the covenant with Israel* that occurs seven years before the Second Coming. The Rapture could have occurred a number of years *before* that. Therefore Gog and Magog could take place some time *after* the Rapture but at least seven years *before* the Great Tribulation starts. Huh??? A fascinating implication of all this is that the Seventieth Week of Daniel, the one supposedly postponed because the Kingdom was postponed and the church age inserted, does *not* begin with the removal of the "parenthesis church" from the world. Why doesn't "Jewish time" start ticking again, as the dispensationalsists used to teach? It's because the Rapture System is still trying to figure out what to do with Gog and Magog.

Simplified Gog

The real solution? Equate Gog and Magog with Armageddon, and the Revelation 19 coming, and Satan's final assault in Revelation 20, and a number of other Old Testament judgement scenes described with battle imagery. Is this really "explaining things away"? I believe it is giving the most credible explanation for a smorgasbord (metaphor!) of prophetic Judgement Day imagery throughout Scripture. It is time to leave the Rapture System behind and make sense of God's prophetic word.

Rapture Woe #11

Rapturists distinguish between the future battles of "Armageddon" and "Gog and Magog" and then in turn conclude, due to "problems" with the timing created by their system, that the "Gog and Magog" battle of Revelation 20:7 must be a different end-times battle from the "Gog and Magog" battle of Ezekiel 38-39. You would think that one "Gog and Magog" would be enough!

14

THE MAN OF LAWLESSNESS

If you are well versed in the Scriptures on the end times and have studied much of what has been said about the Man of Sin/Antichrist/ Beast, you may want to take a deep breath before reading this chapter. It will likely go against most, if not all, of what you have been led to believe about the Man of Lawlessness in 2 Thessalonians 2. I want to be very clear in what I communicate in these next few pages, so that there will be no misunderstanding. After reviewing the printed text on the following page, we will talk through a couple of preliminary issues, and then examine this remarkable passage from God's Word.

Make no mistake about it, 2 Thessalonians is one of the most critical passages of all regarding the end times. All discussions regarding the Antichrist/Beast, Tribulation, Second Coming, etc., go through 2 Thessalonians 2. For many it seems to be the firm foundation for the idea that the church will someday go through a worldwide "Great Tribulation" led by some monstrous ruler out to destroy God's people. This idea may be true. But it may not be. And 2 Thessalonians 2 may, in the final analysis, have nothing to say about the subject!

1 Concerning the coming of our Lord Jesus Christ and our being gathered to him, we ask you, brothers,

2 not to become easily unsettled or alarmed by some prophecy, report or letter supposed to have come from us, saying that the day of the Lord has already come.

3 Don't let anyone deceive you in any way, for that day will not come until the rebellion occurs and the man of lawlessness is revealed, the man doomed to destruction.

4 He will oppose and will exalt himself over everything that is called God or is worshiped, so that he sets himself up in God's temple, proclaiming himself to be God.

5 Don't you remember that when I was with you I used to tell you these things?

6 And now you know what is holding him back, so that he may be revealed at the proper time.

7 For the secret power of lawlessness is already at work; but the one who now holds it back will continue to do so till he is taken out of the way.

8 And then the lawless one will be revealed, whom the Lord Jesus will overthrow with the breath of his mouth and destroy by the splendor of his coming.

9 The coming of the lawless one will be in accordance with the work of Satan displayed in all kinds of counterfeit miracles, signs and wonders,

10 and in every sort of evil that deceives those who are perishing. They perish because they refused to love the truth and so be saved.

11 For this reason God sends them a powerful delusion so that they will believe the lie

12 and so that all will be condemned who have not believed the truth but have delighted in wickedness.

13 But we ought always to thank God for you, brothers loved by the Lord, because from the beginning God chose you to be saved through the sanctifying work of the Spirit and through belief in the truth.

14 He called you to this through our gospel, that you might share in the glory of our Lord Jesus Christ.

15 So then, brothers, stand firm and hold to the teachings we passed on to you, whether by word of mouth or by letter.

16 May our Lord Jesus Christ himself and God our Father, who loved us and by his grace gave us eternal encouragement and good hope,

17 encourage your hearts and strengthen you in every good deed and word.

(2 Thessalonians 2)

A Pivotal Text-A Problem Text

Paul's words here are viewed as weighty and decisive by many Bible scholars and so they should be. But there may be a slight problem. It is possible, and, I believe, likely that, at some point early along the way, the church outside Thessalonica missed the exact point of Paul's rather cryptic prophecy (or "oracle").

Most would agree that this is Paul's most difficult teaching to understand. Because of it, some critics have denied that Paul wrote it! Others have even suggested that 2 Thessalonians was written *before* 1 Thessalonians. Others, who *do* take it for what it claims to be, become very vague and uncertain in their unraveling of the specifics of the text. Perhaps some things were just not meant to be understood, we are told.

Why do commentators struggle so with this chapter? I contend that it is because we have lost the key to unlock the rather vague–perhaps "veiled"–terminology that Paul employs. I believe that a series of false assumptions has led us far from the original intention of the oracle. If I am right, the implications for New Testament eschatology are enormous.

The Pre-trib Dispensational Dilemma

2 Thessalonians 2 opens with a controversy disrupting the church. Some in the church apparently were being led to believe that the Day of the Lord had already occurred or was immediately upon them. If so, they obviously had missed it or had misunderstood what "it" was all about (verses 1-2)! Paul wants to reassure them that the Day of the Lord *has not* taken place, as some deceivers had claimed, and that it *would not* take place until certain events transpired. These events involving the "Man of Lawlessness" and the "rebellion" had been the frequent topic of discussion when Paul had been with them, as he now reminds them (verse 5). The Greek word ELEGON at verse 5 is an imperfect tense verb that denotes continuous past action ("I *used to* tell you ....").

How Relevant?

If we are to believe the Rapturist take on this passage, this ongoing topic of conversation between Paul and the Thessalonians was the career of the end-times Antichrist following the Rapture of the church and preceding the Second (third?) Coming (that would follow the Rapture by seven years). This whole approach is really quite bewildering in view of the much more pressing matters at hand for the beleaguered Thessalonian Christians.

The Rapturists teach that there will be a separate Rapture of the church seven years before Christ's return ("Revelation") to earth. At that Rapture, the saints will be caught up in the air to be with the Lord (using 1 Thessalonians 4). This would also seem to be the "being gathered to him" described here at 2 Thessalonians 2:1. At the later return of Christ to rule on earth, the saints will not rise to meet him in the sky. Of course the problem for the Rapturists is that the language of Scripture in no way supports such a distinction between a "Rapture" and a subsequent "Revelation" of Christ.

Originally, proponents of the separate Rapture of the church attempted to make a distinction between the PAROUSIA ("coming"–referring to the Rapture) and the APOKALYPSIS ("revelation"–referring to the Second Coming). This was later abandoned since it could not be consistently maintained.

Missing the Obvious

If the Thessalonian Christians were concerned that somehow they had missed the "Day of the Lord," that is, the Second Coming *seven years after* the earlier "Rapture," *wouldn't the fact that the Rapture itself hadn't occurred yet be an obvious corrective?* Why bother to discuss the so-called Great Tribulation, along with the alleged Antichrist's career, when the key event that enables the church to "escape" all that stuff obviously hasn't occurred? Why go into detail about a series of events that the Rapture, the so-called "Blessed Hope," would *precede* and would in fact *preclude* Christians from having to experience? If indeed Paul's teaching in 2 Thessalonians 2 is in response to the confusion some are in because false teachers have claimed that the "Day of the Lord" has already happened, the Rapturist interpretation of Paul's words makes no sense whatsoever. The Rapture System's understanding of the role of the Man of Lawlessness in prophecy forces its adherents into a completely illogical line of reasoning here.

More Desperationalism

Of course desperate circumstances require desperate measures. Some Rapturists attempt to save the day here at all costs by holding to an extremely unlikely meaning for the Greek word APOSTASIA at verse 3. This word is variously rendered as "falling away" or "rebellion" by most translators (note our English derivative "apostasy" in the religious sense). In light of the inherent difficulties of holding that Paul here skips over the Rapture and begins discussing the post-Rapture Antichrist, Rapturists actually have tried to argue that the very word APOSTASIA here refers to the Rapture of the church. No kidding! They try to interpret the term in the sense of "departure" and turn it into a *positive* sense. By doing so they now can have Paul making reference to the Rapture in his response to the Thessalonians' concern. Therefore Paul is saying in verse 3, according to them, that the Day of the Lord (Second Coming) will not come until the "Departure" (Rapture) occurs and the Man of Lawlessness (Antichrist) is revealed (3½ years later). This makes sense to Rapturists since it fits their System, but it does not correspond to any reasonable understanding of the word APOSTASIA. The basic sense of "rebellion" for this term is now recognized by our more recent translations (*New International Version, English Standard Version, New Revised Standard Version*). We will see that this meaning is the one that Josephus gives it, as well, in his many uses of the term. To argue that APOSTASIA refers to the "blessed hope" of the church lacks any credibility whatsoever, and top dispensational scholars (e.g., Walvoord) reject that view.

Post-Tribulational Options

The alternative to the above unlikely approach is, rather, that Paul is explaining that certain events must transpire *before* Christ's coming for his church. The "Rapture"/"Day of the Lord" had not yet occurred and *would not* occur until the Man of Lawlessness had come on the scene. Those premillenialists who are "post-tribulational" see this very clearly and argue it persuasively. They see the so-called Great Tribulation as something the church will go through, rather than escape. The Second Coming is *after* ("post") the Great Tribulation. Their approach better explains Paul's line of reasoning in 2 Thessalonians 2.

The amillennialists would agree with the post-trib premillennialists at this one point. There is no separate Rapture of the church followed by a seven-year period, in the middle of which begins the Great Tribulation, etc., etc. Amillennialists teach that Christ will return in glory and triumph for his church (1 Thessalonians 4:13-18; 2 Thessalonians 1:10) while at the same time dealing out retribution to the wicked (2 Thessalonians 1:7-9).

Will the Man of Lawlessness be an end-times figure who will persecute the church? Or perhaps someone or some institution that has been around for a long time? Protestants and others have pointed to the pope for years, while Catholics have fingered heretics and apostates. It might be viewed as a bit of a stretch to view the word "lawless" as the best term for the pope, regardless of how one views his claims to ecclesiastic authority.

The Antichrist Question

We have just noted that not all amillennialists are convinced that there is an end-time individual who will orchestrate a worldwide persecution of the church. Those who *do* accept such a future scenario are heavily influenced by Paul's teaching on the Man of Lawlessness in 2 Thessalonians 2. The fact is that the use of the term "antichrist" in 1 and 2 John can be explained in various ways. John himself claimed that many antichrists had already come (1 John 2:18). He also defined the spirit and teaching of "antichrist" in terms of false claims being made in his own day (perhaps "Gnostic"), namely that Christ had not "come in the flesh" (1 John 4:3; 2 John 7).

As well, the career of the "Beast" in Revelation 13, 17, etc. (also Daniel 7) can be interpreted as something that spans the entire church age. The apocalyptic style of the book of Revelation creates uncertainty as to how literally one should take the "outline of events" depicted in that book. The image of the "Beast" goes through several transitions, sometimes describing a kingdom, sometimes a king or individual. Alleged Old Testament portrayals of the Antichrist's career, e.g. Daniel 11:36-45, are quite dubious, and certainly cannot form the basis of such a view.

So we are left with 2 Thessalonians 2's Man of Lawlessness as an "unmistakeable" Antichrist looming on the future's horizon. Without this ominous personage, the belief in the certainty of such an end-times figure who will persecute the church worldwide is on much shakier ground. **I am convinced that this Man of Lawlessness text has been the deciding factor for many on this issue.** A glance at a number of treatments on the subject of the Great Tribulation and the Antichrist makes clear how big a role 2 Thessalonians 2 really plays.

The BIG Question

But WHAT IF? What if 2 Thessalonians 2 *isn't* describing a future Antichrist figure? What if the Man of Lawlessness *isn't* slain at Christ's return and *doesn't* immediately precede that return? Wouldn't such a conclusion have far-reaching ramifications for the Antichrist issue? I am convinced it would. *And* I am convinced that this surprising alternative in fact describes the true situation. Paul's teaching on the Man of Lawlessness has an entirely different focus than what we have been led to believe. By a series of mistaken assumptions and translators' misdirections, we have been led down the wrong path. This path has produced consternation for about every interpreter of this passage. No one seems to be very convinced or convincing in attempts to decipher this text. Perhaps that is because they are on the wrong track. The passage doesn't make sense because interpreters are trying to place it in a time frame and context where it simply doesn't belong.

Coming up, I will re-analyze certain terms and expressions that commentators and translators have struggled with to the extent that **no persuasive presentation of this text currently exists**. This new analysis will pave the way for a surprising and compelling new understanding of Paul's teachings in 2 Thessalonians 2. Terms under renewed scrutiny include: APOSTASIA; "lawlessness"; God's temple (NAOS); "the restrainer"/ "that which restrains"; at verse 8 the following terms: the "Lord (Jesus)"; "by"; "the splendor" (EPIPHANEIA); "his coming" (PAROUSIA AUTOU)"; also "the lie" (verse 11); and "condemned" (verse 12).

The Missing *Obvious* Answer

Assuming that the Olivet Discourse was known by Paul, and it almost certainly was, SOMETHING IMPORTANT IS MISSING HERE! It is now A.D. 52, and the Thessalonians are worried about missing the Day of the Lord. But remember, Jesus had given ONE CLEAR SIGN that had to occur before He would return– the A.D. 70 destruction of Jerusalem! Why have we missed this? I guess because it's hard to think of ourselves on the other side of Jerusalem's fall. How could the Second Coming occur when Jerusalem's fall, a sign for that generation, had not yet happened?

I am convinced that Paul received even further revelation about this monumentally important event and that 2 Thessalonians 2 is a type of "A.D. 70 oracle". The political ramifications of writing about this may have been troubling. But Paul could have spoken about it more freely. ("I used to tell you ....") The impending fall of Jerusalem is not mentioned elsewhere in Paul's writings except for his mention of the wrath that would come upon the Jews (also written to the Thessalonians!–1 Thessalonians 2:16). To follow this whole argument will take some retooling. Ready?

A New Paradigm: Rethinking Verse 8

It is my intention to cover this matter in greater depth in a future work–*The Man of Lawlessness and the Time of the End.* For now, we can only hit the highlights. The first order of business is to rethink verse 8, since it seems to say that Jesus will destroy the Man of Lawlessness at His Second Coming. This is what the preterists teach and they themselves link this chapter to A.D. 70. But don't forget, preterists believe that the fall of Jerusalem *was* the Second Coming! That is a view that must be rejected. But how do we avoid such a conclusion and still view this as an A.D. 70 oracle?

The *New International Version* reads (extending into verse 9),

> And then the lawless one will be **revealed**, whom the **Lord Jesus** will overthrow with the breath of his mouth and destroy **by the splendor** of **his coming**. (9) **The coming of the lawless one** will be in accordance with the work of Satan ....

Most translations read pretty much the same, so we are about to break some new ground. The key words or words in question are in bold letters. (1) There is a manuscript difference between **Lord** and **Lord Jesus**. The shorter reading "Lord" is attested less, but it is found in every major manuscript family. Many English translations have the shorter form. The significance? The shorter term "Lord" does not necessarily point to Christ and His Second Coming, but could easily signify God's judgement upon Jerusalem. The Jewish historian Josephus said that, through the Roman armies, God sent down "fire from heaven" upon them.

(2) The term "splendor"–EPIPHANEIA– is best translated "manifestation" or "appearance," not "splendor," and *could* refer to the Man of

Lawlessness, not to the Lord (Jesus). In fact a grammatical argument can be made for that. How?

(3) Everyone understands that the PAROUSIA of verse 8 refers to the Lord, while the PAROUSIA of verse 9 refers to the Man of Lawlessness. However, **our translators always "fix" the word order or add a few words** for us, because the Greek word order as it stands *could* be understood to indicate that the "his coming" of verse 8 and the "whose coming" of verse 9 refer to the same individual!

Here is my proposed translation:

> And then the lawless one will be **revealed**, whom **the Lord** will overthrow with the breath of his mouth and will overpower **at the time of** the **appearance** of **his coming** (9) – **whose coming** is according to the working of Satan . . . .

It can't be! But it can. The Greek words go: THE APPEARANCE OF HIS COMING OF WHOM THE COMING IS ACCORDING TO THE WORKING OF SATAN .... The "his" could go either way, but this understanding transforms this new text into one that now makes perfect sense. The Greek dative case of the word "appearance" could either be dative of "means," as has been generally understood, therefore "by," or possibly dative of "time when," as I have taken it here. The change potentially transforms the text. Note that now the Man of Lawlessness is described by all three "coming" terms: APOKALYPTO, EPIPHANEIA, and PAROUSIA, instead of just two (APOKALYPTO, PAROUSIA).

A New Paradigm: Rethinking the Rest

But what about the idea of the "apostasy," the APOSTASIA (verse 3)? Well, the *New International Version* got it right when it rendered it "rebellion," but not for the right reason! Would you believe that the term APOSTASIA and its twin APOSTASIS are **the words regularly used by Josephus to describe the Jewish revolt against Rome!** They occur dozens of times in Josephus, especially in his *War of the Jews*. Commentators have missed the possibility that the term is being used here in its *political*, not religious sense. But what about the context of persecution? Wouldn't that fit the idea of "apostasy" better?

Look again. Try to find the notion of persecution in the Man of Lawlessness section. Try to find *Christians* there! It is starting to look a little suspicious, isn't it?

Seated in God's Temple

One of the problems with viewing the temple (NAOS) of God as symbolic of the church is that the deceptive efforts of the Man of Lawlessness do not seem to be directed toward believers. There is no anti-Christian sentiment expressed; no mention of the persecution of followers of Christ. The targets of this despot's lies are those who *already* have rejected the truth of God (verses 10-12). The activities of the Lawless One seem to involve self-exaltation over God's laws, standards, and worship regulations. They are in opposition to "everything that is called God or is worshiped." The term "everything" is actually masculine in Greek (PANTA). The phrase "that is called God" is rendered in 1 Corinthians 8:5 as "so-called God" in the context of false gods. The Man of Lawlessness will set himself up against every divine authority or standard–"every so-called god or revered thing." In effect he proclaims himself as the divine standard.

Both religious regulations and the laws of the land are under the merciless control of the Man of Lawlessness. Using the Jerusalem temple as his base of operation and claiming exclusive divine authority, "he sets himself up in God's temple, proclaiming himself to be God." The oracular nature of this prophecy may account for some of the lofty language regarding the claims of the Lawless One. No proposed view out there really makes sense in trying to take these words absolutely literally. Regarding the papacy view, the pope doesn't go around calling himself God, does he? Did he ever? As far as the Rapture System goes, what future human figure within even the most bizarre scenario will get away with claiming to be "above all gods"? Will he bump a million or so Hindu deities? Does this affect Islam's Allah? What modern "so-called gods" are we speaking of here? Or is this "deification" attempt directly aimed at Christians? The language in the passage in no way indicates this last suggestion.

I would submit that the time for any human figure succeeding in a world-wide attempt to claim deity is long past. Perhaps my "sanctified imaginater" is just not as active as that of some. Perhaps the Satanic bag of tricks this alleged figure will unleash surpasses anything I can imagine. What Christian group will buy into the idea of a contemporary man being God in the flesh? If, for the sake of example, such end times wonders were unleashed "according to Bible prophecy," wouldn't the fact of the existence of those Biblical warnings curb the blind acceptance of such claims?

Let's get back to what I think Paul was actually talking about. Usurping divine authority is what seems to be in mind in this passage, a concept that some interpreters would seek to apply to the pope. I would instead attach that rebellious activity to a possible first-century candidate for the title the "Lawless One."

Abominations that Desolate

A number of Bible scholars have suggested a connection between the language of this chapter and that of several other key texts, namely (1) the abomination of desolation reference in Matthew 24:15; and (2) the language of Daniel 9:24-27 involving the coming of a "desolator."

Josephus understood the language of Daniel 9 as being fulfilled in the horrible events of A.D. 70 when the murderous zealots took over the temple mount in Jerusalem and slaughtered thousands, even many as they were coming to worship. The huge temple mount structure became their fortress, and the sight of unimaginable atrocities. Describing the scene, Josephus quotes the high priest Ananus as saying,

> "Certainly it had been good for me to die before I had seen the house of God full of so many abominations, or these sacred places, that ought not to be trodden upon at random, filled with the feet of these blood-shedding villains" (*War of the Jews* 4.3.10)

I have become convinced that Jesus' use of "abomination that desolates" may have had reference to *the actions of the Jews themselves* bringing on the desolations at the hand of the Romans. Josephus understood Daniel 9 this way.

> These men, therefore, trampled upon all the laws of men, and laughed at the laws of God; and for the oracles of the prophets, they ridiculed them as the tricks of jugglers; yet did these prophets foretell many things concerning [the rewards of] virtue, and

[punishments of] vice, which when these zealots violated, they occasioned the fulfilling of those very prophecies belonging to their own country; for there was a certain ancient oracle of those men, that the city should then be taken and the sanctuary burnt, by right of war, when a sedition should invade the Jews, and their own hand should pollute the temple of God. Now while these zealots did not [quite] disbelieve these predictions, they made themselves the instruments of their accomplishment. (4.6.3)

And who is there that does not know what the writings of the ancient prophets contain in them, and particularly that oracle which is just now going to be fulfilled upon this miserable city? For they foretold that this city should be then taken when somebody shall begin the slaughter of his own countrymen. And are not both the city and the entire temple now full of the dead bodies of your countrymen? It is God, therefore, **it is God himself who is bringing on this fire**, to purge that city and temple by means of the Romans, **and is going to pluck up this city, which is full of your pollutions."** (6.2.1)

Amazing statements, aren't they? It is hard to imagine a more likely fulfillment of what Paul is describing in 2 Thessalonians 2 than the incredible scenes that unfolded in Jerusalem during the times Josephus describes. But who was the "Lawless One," and what about the "Restrainer" who had to be removed? At this point, only brief comments can be made. More to come at a later date ....

The Lawless One and the Restrainer

It is possible that Josephus names both the Man of Lawlessness and the Restrainer! Josephus describes the zealot leader John of Gischala as being the primary individual responsible for the horrible fate of the city. Regarding John's actions in fleeing his hometown and coming to Jerusalem, Josephus writes,

Thus did this man put a trick upon Titus, not so much out of regard to the seventh day as to his own preservation, for he was afraid lest he should be quite deserted if the city should be taken, and had his hopes of life in that night, and in his flight therein. **Now this was the work of God, who therefore preserved this John, that he might bring on the destruction of Jerusalem** (4.2.3)

Later,

> These harangues of John's corrupted a great part of the
> young men, and puffed them up for the war; but as to the more
> prudent part, and those in years, there was not a man of them
> but foresaw what was coming, and made lamentation on that ac-
> count, as if the city was already undone; and in this confusion
> were the people. (4.3.1)

Read Josephus to find out about John's arrogance and deception, and
his sacrilege of the temple and the things of God. Hundreds of thousands
died directly because of his lawless despotic behavior.

The "restrainer"? The high priest Ananus. The "restraining thing"?
(Paul uses both the masculine–"the one who restrains"– and the neu-
ter–"that which restrains"–forms.) The functioning Jerusalem priesthood
and temple system. Once these were gone, the Man of Lawlessness clearly
had arrived on the scene and Jerusalem and its inhabitants were doomed.
Josephus writes,

> I should not mistake if I said that the death of Ananus was the
> beginning of the destruction of the city, and that from this very
> day may be dated the overthrow of her wall, and the ruin of her
> affairs, whereon they saw their high priest, and the procurer of
> their preservation, slain in the midst of their city.
>
> ... and I cannot but think that it was because God had
> doomed this city to destruction, as a polluted city, and was re-
> solved to purge his sanctuary by fire, that he cut off these their
> great defenders and well-wishers, while those that a little before
> had worn the sacred garments, and had presided over the public
> worship; and had been esteemed venerable by those that dwelt on
> the whole habitable earth when they came into our city, were cast
> out naked, and seen to be the food of dogs and wild beasts. And I
> cannot but imagine that virtue itself groaned at these men's case,
> and lamented that she was here so terribly conquered by wicked-
> ness. And this at last was the end of Ananus and Jesus. (4.5.2)

What better end-times fulfillment could be provided than what Josephus describes for us in connection with the A.D. 70 fall of Jerusalem?

The Appearance of His Coming

Another argument against verse 8's referring to Jesus' glorious return is that nothing else in the remainder of 2 Thessalonians refers to

it. After what I view as a dative of "time when"–"*at* the appearance of his coming"– everything that follows speaks of the coming (PAROUSIA) of the Lawless One and the deception that will be wrought upon those who have already rejected the truth of the gospel. There is nothing after 2 Thessalonians 2:3 that even hints at a description of the Second Coming except verse 8.

We are told earlier that the Second Coming will not occur unless the Man of Lawlessness first arrives on the scene (verse 3). When he arrives, he will be removed by the breath of the Lord's mouth (verse 8). This could very naturally be interpreted as God's overthrow of Jerusalem and the rebellion at the hands of the Romans. Josephus repeatedly connected Rome's attack upon the city with the exercising of God's wrath. The city and the temple were being consumed by the very "fire of God" (5.2.1). If my understanding of the "*his* coming" at verse 8 be accepted, the entire chapter then makes perfect sense. It offers a very natural answer to the Thessalonians' question in light of what Jesus had taught about the one "sign" that would precede his return in glory.

Understood in this way, 2 Thessalonians 2 does not describe the Second Coming, only the necessary events that would *precede* that coming. As Jesus had taught, once the judgement upon Jerusalem had transpired, no further signs would be given to warn of his return– and clearly *the events of A.D. 70 and the occasion of his personal return were portrayed as distinct occurrences in Jesus' descriptions.* The desolations of A.D. 70 would be preceded by specific warning signs, his glorious return would not.

The verses following verse 8 tell us the following. (1) The Lawless One's coming would be according to the working of Satan (verse 9). (2) Satan's work would involve miracles, lying wonders and wicked deception (verses 9-10). (3) This deception would be directed toward those who have *already* rejected the truth of the gospel (verse 11). (4) God himself would be the one who sends them a delusion– a delusion that would result in their believing "the lie" (verse 11). Satan serves as the unwitting instrument of God's judgment. (5) The result of their believing "the lie" would be that ALL those who had not believed might be condemned (verse 12).

At this point Paul expresses his gratitude for the faith and sanctification of the Thessalonian Christians (verse 13), but there is no further reference to Christ's return. No flaming fire, no coming in glory, no deliverance of the saints, no attending angels, nothing. If 2 Thessalonians 2:8 is a Second Coming reference, it is a remarkably abrupt one! **Instead, everything that follows verse 8 focuses upon the disastrous results of the coming (PAROUSIA) or appearing (EPIPHANEIA) of the Man of Lawlessness.**

This supports the previous arguments given that 2 Thessalonians 2 is not a Second Coming passage at all. Rather it is a passage describing in rather veiled, cryptic and, some might argue, "apocalyptic" language the scene that is about to played out in Jerusalem. Jesus' predictions about Jerusalem's destruction would certainly unfold before "the coming of the Son of Man" occurred. The Thessalonians had forgotten that one paramount sign. No PAROUSIA of Christ would take place until all the things prophesied about "this generation" had come about–until the Jewish APOSTASIA has run its fatal course.

One question that can now be better understood is why is it necessary for the unbelieving wicked to believe "the lie" (TO PSEUDEI)? Aren't they already under God's condemnation? What further lie would be necessary to be believed in order for the unrighteous to be condemned (KRITHOSIN)?

If this refers to eternal punishment, the sense of the text is unclear. However, if it refers to the events in connection with A. D. 70, it makes perfect sense. That evil generation would need to buy into the seditious rebellion against Rome in order for it to be utterly devastated. Amazingly, many thousands of Jews entered Jerusalem at the last moment to celebrate Passover, *even while the Romans were surrounding the city, and even after many thousands had been slain on the temple mount by these murderous revolutionaries!*

The lie that John of Gischala and his followers promoted was that God would never allow the city and temple to fall into Roman hands. No matter what brand of evil these wicked Jews practiced, God would protect them from enemy hands. John commissioned false prophets to propagate that lie, while drawing more and more victims to the temple mount (6.5.2) **As a result of that monstrous lie, hundreds of thousands met their violent end.** Josephus gives the figure at 1,100,000 dead and 97,000 prisoners.

I believe that Paul had already alluded to the upcoming horrors of A.D. 70 in his *first* letter to the Thessalonians (2:14-16).

> For you, brothers, became imitators of God's churches in Judea, which are in Christ Jesus: You suffered from your own countrymen the same things those churches suffered from the Jews, who killed the Lord Jesus and the prophets and also drove us out. They displease God and are hostile to all men in their effort to keep us from speaking to the Gentiles so that they may be saved. **In this way they always heap up their sins to the limit. The wrath of God has come upon them at last.**

Jesus himself had earlier said to the corrupt Jewish leaders of his day (Matthew 23:35-38):

> And so upon you will come all the righteous blood that has been shed on earth, from the blood of righteous Abel to the blood of Zechariah son of Berekiah, whom you murdered between the temple and the altar. I tell you the truth, **all this will come upon this generation. O Jerusalem, Jerusalem, you who kill the prophets and stone those sent to you,** how often I have longed to gather your children together, as a hen gathers her chicks under her wings, but **you were not willing. Look, your house is left to you desolate.**

How fitting that the desolation wrought upon Jerusalem was caused by that wicked generation itself, as the descriptions by Josephus so vividly portray. The Man of Lawlessness and his seditious accomplices played their role to the hilt in a deadly drama orchestrated by God in fulfillment of our Lord's tearful words. The LIE was believed. The destruction was complete– a horrific desolation brought in connection with the unspeakable abominations committed by the Man of Lawlessness and his followers.

Rapture Woe #12

Rapturists actually have tried to argue that the word APOSTASIA in 2 Thessalonians 2 refers to the Rapture of the church! They try to interpret the term in the sense of "departure" rather than "rebellion." By doing so they now can have Paul making reference to the Rapture in his response to the Thessalonians' concern. This is another case of "desperationalism" and again demonstrates that 1 Thessalonians 4 does not teach a separate Rapture.

The Rapture Has Been

Due to Lack
of Scriptural Evidence

In the course of this book, the Rapture System has been analyzed in view of its main teachings and assumptions. The heart of the system, the sharp distinction between Israel and the church was found to be unjustified. The Postponement Theory dates from around 1830 and teaches that the Kingdom promises were postponed when the Messiah was rejected by the Jewish nation. In its place the church was added, a kind of "Plan B." It is often referred to as the "parenthesis church." Based on this theory, the Seventieth Week of Daniel is viewed as postponed as well, in which they envision an Antichrist figure who will persecute the Jews and destroy Jerusalem.

Actually, Daniel was talking about the A.D. 70 destruction, and the seventieth week instead featured the atoning work of the Messiah. The *New International Version* here was obviously produced by a Rapturist at Daniel 9:27, and misleading words are added, e.g., the phrase "he will set up," which is *not* italicized but should be, has been supplied for our "understanding." The original does not include or hint at these words. As well, the word "abomination" is actually plural, "abominations." Translation cannot help but supply interpretation at times, but the *NIV* goes too far in this instance.

The Postponement Cancelled

The Postponement Theory is so contrary to the teachings of the New Testament that many dispensationalists have been trying to find some new middle– and, so far, rocky– ground. The Old Testament *did* prophesy the church age and therefore promises to the nation of Israel are being fulfilled in the New Testament church. Once the postponement is refuted, the basis for the postponement of the Seventieth Week of Daniel becomes even less valid. Without that postponed week, many assumptions about the meaning of the 3½ / 42 months / 1260 days in Revelation weaken dramatically. They need not represent a literal 3½ years. These numbers may just represent the experiences of the church from the perspective of testing or persecution, as the context and flow of Revelation would suggest. If the Olivet Discourse is given a logical, reasoned reading, much of the evidence for the Great Tribulation and Abomination of Desolation events disappears from the end-times horizon.

My solution to the Man of Lawlessness mystery may not be embraced by all. It is no doubt a shock to the system for many. Either way, however, 2 Thessalonians 2 flies in the face of any attempt to read a separate Rapture of the church into the future scene. The APOSTASIA is *not* the Rapture! For those who reject my approach to 2 Thessalonians 2, the problem of the denial of the imminence of Christ's return remains, unless one opts for a more generalizing, continuing fulfillment for the Man of Lawlessness language. Unfortunately, such an approach runs the risk of making the fulfillment so vague that it doesn't function effectively as a sign, as it seems to do in Paul's vivid description.

The Rapture Really *Is* Secret

The "secret" Rapture is in fact well named. You can't find it anywhere in the Bible! Perhaps the "hidden" Rapture would be better. Dispensationalists admit a lack of texts where both the Rapture and the Revelation are clearly mentioned and distinguished. A favorite attempt is Titus 2:

13–"the blessed hope and glorious appearing," as if those were separated by seven years. The *New International Version* doesn't see it that way, as it reads "while we wait for the blessed hope– the glorious appearing of our great God and Savior, Jesus Christ." The Rapture doctrine derives from the "system" more than from specific biblical statements.

The Big Three

In his book, *The Rapture*, LaHaye refers to three main Rapture passages: John 14:1-3; 1 Corinthians 15:51-58; and 1 Thessalonians 4:13-18. Just to read the texts is virtually to dismiss these claims.

Rapture Text #1

> Do not let your hearts be troubled. Trust in God; trust also in me. In my Father's house are many rooms; if it were not so, I would have told you. I am going there to prepare a place for you. And if I go and prepare a place for you, I will come back and take you to be with me that you also may be where I am. (John 14:1-3)

At the Lord's return, He will come to take us "home" to be with Him. I'm sorry, but this is not a clear separate-Rapture text. How could anyone ever say that it is?

Rapture Text #2

> Listen, I tell you a mystery: We will not all sleep, but we will all be changed– 52 in a flash, in the twinkling of an eye, at the last trumpet. For the trumpet will sound, the dead will be raised imperishable, and we will be changed. 53 For the perishable must clothe itself with the imperishable, and the mortal with immortality. 54 When the perishable has been clothed with the imperishable, and the mortal with immortality, then the saying that is written will come true: "Death has been swallowed up in victory." 55 "Where, O death, is your victory? Where, O death, is your sting?" 56 The sting of death is sin, and the power of sin is the law. 57 But thanks be to God! He gives us the victory through our Lord Jesus Christ. 58 Therefore, my dear brothers, stand firm. Let nothing move you. Always give yourselves fully to the work of the Lord, because you know that your labor in the Lord is not in vain. (1 Corinthians 15:51-58)

What a great text. At the last trumpet ... we shall all be changed! But wait. Where's the separate Rapture? Still a secret, apparently. This cannot be claimed as evidence for the pre-trib (or any-trib) Rapture of the church. One to go ....

Rapture Text #3

> We believe that Jesus died and rose again and so we believe that God will bring with Jesus those who have fallen asleep in him. According to the Lord's own word, we tell you that we who are still alive, who are left till **the coming of the Lord**, will certainly not precede those who have fallen asleep. For **the Lord himself will come down from heaven, with a loud command, with the voice of the archangel and with the trumpet call of God**, and the dead in Christ will rise first. After that, we who are still alive and are left will be **caught up together with them in the clouds to meet the Lord in the air**. And so we will be with the Lord forever. Therefore encourage each other with these words. (1 Thessalonians 4:14-18)

Another beautiful scene, but note how loud this secret coming will be! Jesus did say, "Let him who has ears to hear, let him hear," so maybe only the elect will hear that Rapture trumpet blowing. Fine, but no separate Rapture is clearly taught here. In fact, Rapturists struggle with the wording of the very next chapter, for although the topic has not seemed to change, this "thief in the night" coming is said to be accompanied by God's punishment upon the wicked. Not so "separate" after all.

> Now, brothers, about times and dates we do not need to write to you, for you know very well that **the day of the Lord will come like a thief in the night**. While people are saying, "Peace and safety," **destruction will come on them suddenly**, as labor pains on a pregnant woman, and they will not escape. But you, brothers, are not in darkness so that this day should surprise you like a thief. (1 Thessalonians 5:1)

Another "thief" text creates even more problems, because an intervening "Millennium" on earth is not pictured before the New Heaven and New Earth is created when He comes. 2 Peter 3:10-13 reads,

> But **the day of the Lord** will come like a **thief**. The heavens will disappear with a roar; the elements will be destroyed by fire, and the earth and everything in it will be laid bare. Since everything will be destroyed in this way, what kind of people ought you to be? You ought to live holy and godly lives as you look forward to **the day of God** and speed its coming. **That day will bring about the destruction of the heavens by fire, and the elements will melt in the heat.**

But in keeping with his promise we are looking forward to a new heaven and a new earth, the home of righteousness.

Obscure or Not?

None of LaHaye's top three texts pass the test. What else is there? In his chapter, "Who Says It's Obscure?" (in his book, *The Rapture*), LaHaye seeks to deflect this criticism by claiming to have found the Rapture in "one verse, one chapter, and one book." Interesting approach, isn't it? So what are we talking about here?

One Verse

The one verse is Titus 2:13 regarding "the blessed hope and glorious appearing" of Jesus Christ. I hope you weren't hoping for a more persuasive verse. There is no help here for the Rapture, and not much hope of finding any elsewhere.

One Chapter

The "one chapter" amazingly, is 2 Thessalonians 2, where LaHaye argues that the "gathering together to him" refers to the Rapture. I refer you to my chapter "The Man of Lawlessness." Paul's teaching on the Man of Lawlessness makes no sense if, as LaHaye believes, he appears on the scene *after* the Rapture of the church. This chapter actually refutes, not supports, the Rapture.

One Book

Revelation is supposed to be the "one book" that teaches the separate Rapture of the church. But this is an interpretation based on the dispensational spin on the book, not on any clear teaching. Remarkably, LaHaye and other Rapturists believe that Revelation 4-18 (or 6-18) describes the seven years between the Rapture and the Second Coming. After the letters to the churches in chapters 2-3, the church gets pretty much left out of this book. This would be the direct opposite emphasis from that which the new insights on apocalyptic literature would suggest. Where's the Rapture here? Well, Revelation says that John was taken up into heaven (4:1-2). Remember that dispensationalists are supposed to take things literally, but here they are willing to make an exception! The church is represented by John. He is "raptured" as a symbol of the church. Who says the Rapture is "obscure"?

The Bottom Line

Perhaps the words of Hal Lindsey in his *The Late Great Planet Earth* are the most revealing as to the "bottom line" in all this. In giving evidence for the separate Rapture he admits,

> Here is the chief reason why we believe the Rapture occurs before the Tribulation: the prophets have said that God will set up a Kingdom on earth over which the Messiah will rule. There will be mortal people in that kingdom. If the Rapture took place at the same time as the second coming, there would be no mortals who would be believers; therefore, there would be no one to go into the Kingdom and repopulate the earth. (p. 143)

Rapture Woe #13

The "secret" Rapture is in fact well named. You can't find it anywhere in the Bible! Perhaps the "hidden" Rapture would be better. Dispensationalists admit a lack of texts where both the Rapture and the Revelation are clearly distinguished. No convincing text can be provided.

The message is clear. The Rapture is a product of the "System," the hyperliteral dispensational premillennial approach. No real evidence for the Rapture exists.

Many other texts are cited as Rapture texts by proponents of the Rapture System. But the real bottom line remains the same. They all can be read simply as Second Coming texts. You see, the "blessed hope" is not escape from the Beast, it is being received by Christ in glory.

The doctrine of the Second Coming is a wonderful source of comfort for Christians who long to be with Christ as Paul did (Philippians 1: 23). The redemption of this fallen creation and of our mortal bodies will be a marvelous day (Romans 8:19-23). The Scripture's teaching on the Second Coming of Christ is "sensational" enough without the current marketing efforts of Rapture Mania.

The Bible's teachings are clear. The future developments of current world events are not. Should we be solid interpreters of the Word, or political prognosticators of a rapidly changing world? To the testimony! Let's be diligent in our handling rightly the Word of Truth. It's time for the church to move on. Leave the Rapture behind.

Epilogue:

Book of Woes

RAPTURE WOE # 1

The separate "Rapture" of the church offers a second chance for those who are "left behind" then to accept Christ and enter the "Millennial Kingdom."

RAPTURE WOE # 2

Their "postponement" theory teaches that Christ's church, rather than being central in God's plans, was merely an "afterthought" brought about by the Jewish rejection of the kingdom. One might conclude that Christ, then, apparently failed in His mission when He came into the world, in that He came to establish the "Kingdom."

RAPTURE WOE # 3

Rapturists' hyperliteral interpretation leads to a bizarre, complex sequence of future events and ignores the way in which the New Testament interprets many of the Old Testament prophecies.

RAPTURE WOE # 4

At the very time more and more church-goers are jumping on to the traditional pre-trib Rapture bandwagon, many of the best and brightest within the dispensational fold are having second thoughts about some of the basic assumptions of that system. A new movement calling itself Progressive Dispensationalism is sending shockwaves throughout the Rapture System's realm.

RAPTURE WOE # 5

Paul taught that a "remnant" from Israel–the elect throughout the ages–would be saved, not some future generation after the Rapture of the church.

RAPTURE WOE # 6

There are no land promises to Abraham that must yet be fulfilled. "Solomon ruled over all the kingdoms from the River to the land of the Philistines and to the border of Egypt ..." (I Kings 4:21). In fact, he had dominion over "everything west of the River" (I Kings 4:24).

RAPTURE WOE # 7

The promised conversion of the Gentiles began its fulfillment in the first century efforts of the New Testament Christians. This was in fulfillment of the promises to David. No future Millennial Kingdom is needed for a fulfillment.

RAPTURE WOE # 8

The use of typological language for messianic prophecy means that military-sounding "conquests" actually refer to the spiritual conquest of the nations–their conversion, that is. The "New David" will do "David-like" things. Future military conquests for Israel are not what the Bible is describing.

RAPTURE WOE # 9

The more careful Rapturists teach that the left behind" texts are not talking about the Rapture at all, but rather the later Revelation, and that those left behind are actually the righteous, not the wicked!

RAPTURE WOE # 10

Descriptions of the eternal New Jerusalem in the Old Testament are claimed by dispensationalists to refer instead to the "millennial" city, in spite of clear parallels with the eternal city of Revelation 21-22. The Rapturist claim to the normal, natural meaning of words does not always stand up under careful investigation. Terminology in the Old Testament that the Rapture System claims for the Millennium is the same used in the New for the Eternal State.

RAPTURE WOE # 11

Rapturists distinguish between the future battles of "Armageddon" and "Gog and Magog" and then in turn conclude, due to "problems" with the timing their system creates, that the "Gog and Magog" battle of Revelation 20:7 must be a different end-times battle from the "Gog and Magog" battle of Ezekiel 38-39. You would think that one "Gog and Magog" would be enough!

RAPTURE WOE # 12

Rapturists actually have tried to argue that the word APOSTASIA in 2 Thessalonians 2 refers to the Rapture of the church! They try to interpret the term in the sense of "departure" rather than "rebellion." By doing so they now can have Paul making reference to the Rapture in his response to the Thessalonians' concern. This is another case of "desperationalism" and again demonstrates that 1 Thessalonians 4 does not teach a separate Rapture.

RAPTURE WOE # 13

The "secret" Rapture is in fact well named. You can't find it anywhere in the Bible! Perhaps the "hidden" Rapture would be better. Dispensationalists admit a lack of texts where both the Rapture and the Revelation are clearly distinguished. No convincing text can be provided.

Let's add one more WOE:

RAPTURE WOE #14

The chief argument for the Rapture, according to Hal Lindsey: the prophets have said that God will set up a Kingdom on earth over which the Messiah will rule. It is a matter of presupposition, not of Scriptural evidence. THERE IS NO BIBLICAL EVIDENCE FOR THE SEPARATE RAPTURE OF THE CHURCH.

For Further Research

Non-dispensational Works

Allis, Oswald T. *Prophecy and the Church*. Philadelphia: Presbyterian and Reformed Publishing Company, 1947.

Bales, James D. *New Testament Interpretation of Kingdom Prophecies*. Searcy, Arkansas: The Harding College Press, 1950.

Butler, Paul. *Approaching the New Millennium: An Amillennial Look at A.D. 2000*. Joplin, Missouri: College Press Publishing Company, 19998.

Clouse, Robert G. (ed.). *The Meaning of the Millenium: Four Views*. Downers Grove, Illinois: InterVarsity Press,1979.

Cox, William E. *Amillennialism Today*. Philadelphia: Presbyterian and Reformed Publishing Company, 1972.

_____. *Biblical Studies In Final Things*. Philadelphia: Presbyterian and Reformed Publishing Company, 1972.

_____. *An Examination of Dispensationalism*. Philadelphia: Presbyterian and Reformed Publishing Company, 1971.

Friskney, Tom. *Strength for Victory: A Commentary on the Book of Revelation*. 1986.

Grier, W. J. *The Momentous Event*. London: The Banner of Truth Trust, 1970.

Gundry, Robert H. *The Church and the Tribulation*. Grand Rapids: Zondervan Publishing House, 1973.

Moore, Mark E. *How to Dodge a Dragon*. Joplin, Missouri: College Press Publishing Company, 1998.

Kik, J. Marcellus. *An Eschatology of Victory*. Philadelphia: Presbyterian and Reformed Publishing Company, 1971.

Kyle, Richard. *The Last Days are Here Again*. Grand Rapids: Baker Books, 1998.

Ladd, George E. *Jesus and the Kingdom*. Waco, Texas: Word Books, 1964.

MacPherson, Dave. *The Unbelievable Pre-Trib Origin*. Kansas City, Missouri: Heart of America Bible Society, 1973.

Paher, Stanley W. *The Book of Revelation's Mystery Babylon Rome, A D. 95.* Reno, Nevada: Nevada Publications, 2003.

Mauro, Philip. *The Hope of Israel.* Swengel, Pennsylvania: Reiner Publications, 1970.

_____. *The Seventy Weeks and the Great Tribulation.* Swengel, Pennsylvania: Reiner Publications, n.d.

Smith, James E. "The Fall of Babylon: A Problem in Prophetic Interpretation," *The Seminary Review* (The Cincinnati Bible Seminary) 17 (Fall, 1970), 2-23.

_____. *What the Bible Says About the Promised Messiah.* Kissimmee, Florida: Restoration Press, 1991.

Dispensational Works

Aldrich, Willard M. "The Interpretation of Acts 15:13-18," *Bibliotheca Sacra* 111 (October, 1954), 317-323.

Bateman IV, Herbert W. (ed.). *Three Central Issues in Contemporary Dispensationalism.* Grand Rapids, Michigan: Kregel Publications, 1999.

Blaising, Craig A. and Darrell L. Bock. *Progressive Dispensationalism.* USA: A Bridge Point Book, 1993.

Blaising, Craig A. and Darrell L Bock (eds). *Dispensationalism, Israel and the Church: The Search of Definition.* Grand Rapids, Michigan; Zondervan Publishing House, 1992.

Dellaan, Richard. *Israel and the Nations.* Grand Rapids: Zondervan publishing House, 1971.

Ice, Thomas and Kenneth L. Gentry Jr. *The Great Tribulation: Past of Future?* Grand Rapids, Michigan: Kregel Publications,1999. [A debate between dispensationalism and preterism]

Ironside, H. A. *The Lamp of Prophecy.* Grand Rapids: Zondervan Publishing House, 1940.

Jeffrey, Grant R. *Triumphant Return: The Coming Kingdom of God.* Toronto, Ontario: Frontier Research Publication, Inc., 2001.

LaHaye, Tim. *Understanding Bible Prophecy for Yourself.* Eugene, Oregon: Harvest House Publishers, 2001.

LaHaye, Tim and Thomas Ice. *Charting the End Times.* Eugene, Oregon: Harvest House Publishers, 2001.

_____. *The End Times Controversy.* Eugene, Oregon: Harvest House Publishers, 2003.

LaHaye, Tim and Jerry B. Jenkins. *Are We Living in the End Times?* Wheaton, Illinois: Tyndale House Publishers, Inc., 1999.

Lindsey, Hal. *The Late Great Planet Earth*. Grand Rapids: Zondervan Publishing House, 1970.

Pentecost, J. Dwight. *Things To Come*. Grand Rapids: Zondervan Publishing House, 1964.

Saucy, Robert L. *The Case For Progressive Dispensationalism*. Grand Rapids, Michigan: Zondervan Publishing House, 1993.

Scofield, C. I. *The Scofield Reference Bible*. New York: Oxford University Press, 1917.

Walvoord, John F. *Israel in Prophecy*. Grand Rapids: Zondervan Publishing House, 1970.

_____. *The Millennial Kingdom*. Grand Rapids: Zondervan Publishing House, 1959.

Wood, Leon J. *The Bible and Future Events*. Grand Rapids: Zondervan Publishing House, 1973.

For information about obtaining

Leaving the Rapture Behind

go to

www.leavingtheraprurebehind.com

or write

MIREH Publishers
P. O. Box 1376
Joplin, MO 64802